The Moments That Make Us

PETE EVICK

The Moments That Make Us

PETE EVICK

Crossroads Publishing House

The Moments That Make Us

Copyright © 2015, Pete Evick

Print ISBN: 978-0692288139

Cover Art Design by Keith Sarna

Release Date, June 16, 2015

Crossroads Publishing House

P.O. Box 55

Pfafftown, NC 27040

Special thanks to...

Bret Michaels
Kristen Johns
Gavin Evick
Jacob Evick
Sylvia Haydash
Cyndi Stephens
Sherry Hoover
Nancy Naigle
Tina Lu
Scott Cohen
Ron Bienstock
Daniel A. Weiss
Keith Sarna

This book is for my two amazing children,
Gavin and Jacob,
who have given me all the reason in the world to be the
best man I can be. Without the love I have for them, I'd
never have been able to complete the journey that
resulted in me writing this book.

.

LETTER TO THE READER

Soul-searching, self-reflection, or life evaluation—whatever you call it in this day and age, it's a common and necessary practice.

The world we live in is fast paced, cutthroat, and incredibly confusing. We are often forced to make choices we truly aren't sure about, or weren't ready to make. We spend our time saying "What if?" or "I shouldn't have." We often look out instead of in as we try to find the root of what makes us tick, placing blame on everyone and everything other than ourselves along the way.

My name is Pete Evick. I'm a forty-two-year-old musician, producer, songwriter, and, apparently now, an author.

I've spent the better part of a decade soul-searching, and every second of the last five years in deep self-reflection, trying desperately to find out why I am who I am, and how to ensure that my precious children don't end up the confused and twisted adult their father is. I've come to realize that every single breath you take, every word you hear, and everything you see as a child plays a part in the adult you become. I've found that the simplest things, some of which happened before I was born, and some that may never happen at all, were crucial building blocks in my character.

I certainly don't have all the answers, but I

write this book as a call to those who are ready to retrace their paths and peek beneath unturned stones to find themselves.

Hopefully my stories will be unique enough examples of the oddest places in which I've found *me*, that they will convince *you* to dig a little deeper into your own mind and soul.

It was my original hope that this book would inspire broken families to find a way back to the love that originally brought them together. But as I began to write, I realized what I wanted to share was applicable to many situations and much deeper than I originally suspected.

What I have to say applies to couples who are still together, couples who truly are better off apart, teachers, preachers, Scout leaders, aunts, uncles, and every single person who influences us as children. It's about how very careful we must be with the so easily influenced mind of a child. That innocent, smiling kid can take a simple glance, word, or action and carry it with them subconsciously into their adult life.

I'm well aware that my views may not win the popular vote. I just hope to evoke the mental archaeologist lying dormant in all of us.

Pete Evick

Foreword
By Scott Cohen
Founder, The Orchard
Music Manager and Industry Visionary

It seems that every rock star and musician writes a book these days. They try to dazzle us with their tales of sex, drugs, and rock and roll. Massive egos, playing by their own rules. "Look at how amazing I am." Yawn. Give me a break.

Pete Evick is a real rock star. A talented guitar player and songwriter with the grit and determination to succeed. And all the while fumbling through life just trying to figure out how to do the best for his family and friends. No different than you and me. But very different from the ego-driven world of rock and roll because he opens up his heart and tells all. Not tells all about other people—tells all about his insecurities, character flaws, innermost hopes, and his journey to be a better person.

I remember the first time I met Pete. He was just a teenager in a little local band that wanted a chance to open for a larger act I was managing. He was persistent. I couldn't say no, and that has been a common theme in our relationship for the last twenty-five years. "Yes, Pete. For you, anything." How does he do it?

For all these years I have watched from the bleachers like a proud father watching his son play sports. Rooting Pete on. I remember getting an email from him once when he was on tour. He was worried that he would never "make it." I told him something along the lines of "Are you fucking crazy? You are playing to thousands of people a night. You are doing exactly what you love. And the people love you. Take a moment to recognize this. Enjoy the fact that you *have* made it."

Looking back, maybe I misunderstood the question. Of course, Pete made it as a rock star. But did he "make it" as a man? As a son? A husband? A friend? A father? How do you even measure that? I don't know, but let me give it a shot.

Pete made mistakes in his life like everybody else. What makes him the man he is today is his willingness to take a hard look at his life, understand where he fucked up, and try to change. Sounds easy, but it might be the hardest thing in life to do.

I'm honored that I get to follow along on Pete's journey and thrilled that he has decided to share it with others.

Proud as ever,
Scott Cohen

Chapter One
Who, What, When, and Why?

As a musician, I've been blessed with the gift of being able to provide a good life for my children by playing loud rock-and-roll music all over the world, but after a decade of marriage, I was faced with the breakup of my family. While not my choice, it was certainly my doing. Don't misunderstand me. Though I didn't realize it at the time, my wife was patient and it was me who drove her far enough away that trying to fix what we once had together wasn't even an option. It's hard to believe you can drive someone who loves you that far away without even knowing it, but I'm living proof.

Divorce might seem like no big deal to most people these days. Call me old-fashioned, but I desperately wanted to keep my family intact. While I simply do not believe in divorce, I'm wise enough to know that sometimes you have to do what you don't want to. I am compassionate enough to understand that if you love someone you must set them free. But...that was a hard lesson to learn.

It got to the point that my career took me out on the road for nine months out of the year, and when I was home I was so exhausted I couldn't function. The simple task of taking the trash out seemed like slave labor. People often wonder, what is so exhausting about playing guitar for ninety minutes a night? This question used to work me up so bad, it's not that ninety minutes is that long, it's the rest of the day. There's much more to putting on a show than just the time that I'm on stage. Traveling is exhausting; living out of a backpack or suitcase is exhausting. Imagine having to set your office up and tear it down every single day. Now imagine having to also set up your personal and hygienic needs every day. Checking into a room, putting out your razor, shampoo, and toothbrush. You basically start over on a daily basis. Yet . . . make no mistake, it is also amazing, exciting, and unexplainable. I dreamed about it, I craved it, and I wouldn't change a thing, but it is exhausting and all consuming. You've heard the expression, "I need a vacation, from my vacation." It's a lot like that after nine months on the road.

And what kind of life is that for the person waiting at home for you? Waiting for you to go out and do things, experience life, make memories, and you can't find the energy to get off the couch.

When you have children, though, divorce becomes more complicated and the children's happiness and well-being must—or at least *should*—be considered.

So, I won't lie. I selfishly tried to save my marriage.

I played the do-it-for-the-kids card.

And to that, for those of you who have been involved in the division of a family, I'm sure you've heard this phrase before:

Kids are resilient.

Be it from your parents, your therapist, or whomever you have confided in, you have without a doubt been met with that phrase.

In fact, the original title of this book was going to be

Kids Are Resilient . . .
But What about the Adults We Become?

But as I neared completion it was obvious I had written something completely different.

That phrase has to be the biggest cliché in the world of break-ups. It's said only to soothe the guilt and pain of the parents who are choosing to take this path.

Kids are resilient, no doubt about it. The problem is that, the adults we become, more times than not, are twisted and broken.

We end up in therapy for years far into our adult life; misinterpreting our therapists and convincing ourselves week after week that we have every right to blame our parents for every bad choice we've ever made, every failed relationship we've had, and every tear we've shed. It's like the mantra of the twenty-first-century adult has become "Take Responsibility for Nothing."

Interestingly enough, one of the biggest disagreements my wife and I had post separation was her feeling that I wasn't taking any responsibility for what happened. In my head, I had clearly owned up to and admitted all of my mistakes both to her and her family, as well as publicly to people who weren't even involved. But in my journey, I searched for the reasons why I did the things I did, and that was the key to what drove me to write this book and share my experiences.

There's a fine line between reason and blame. For example, if I say to you that I don't like mayonnaise, I'll find myself wondering why I don't. I dig for the root cause. If I come to the conclusion that it's because my dad always had it on his lip while eating his lunch and it freaked me out, then in my mind I've found the reason. But to me it's not about placing blame or making an excuse, it's just the reason. I don't feel any anger toward my dad that it's because of him I can't stand mayonnaise. It simply explains my reaction.

Everything in life affects us. Some for the good, and some not so much.

Even when someone says something more positive like, "You play guitar well," I will again search and wonder why I ended up good at that particular thing. I develop a list of teachers and reasons why I succeeded in that part of my life. Despite the positive or negative outcome, to me it's the same math as I described above; I use the same formula to search for an answer.

I could hardly imagine someone challenging or debating with me for giving a reason why I ended up doing well at something, but when I give a reason why I failed at something, then all of a sudden they get mad and I'm accused of not owning my mistakes. It sure is a head trip to perceive it that way, don't you think?

In the end, though, perception is everything. As humans, we can't even prove that what my eyes perceive as red is what your eyes see as red. Yet we are so self-centered that we often truly assume everyone feels, thinks, and should act the way we do.

It's simply not the case.

From something as basic as our taste buds to

something as complex as our sexual preferences, we are each worlds apart in what makes us tick. When we realize this and start trying to accept, not change, other people's perceptions, I can guarantee you that we will start seeing a lot less of the negative stuff in our personal lives and the world around us.

The Beatles weren't too far off when they sang "All you need is love." The difference is that we need unconditional love, and the truth is, most of us haven't come close to understanding what that truly is yet. We eventually have to start looking at the world differently or we will remain right where we are—stalling our evolution in its tracks.

It's my belief that our next step as a species is a combination of communication and perception.

I have a vague memory of seeing this guy talk on television as a kid. I don't remember exactly if he was a comedian, a newscaster, if it was a sitcom or a talk show; however, in my brain the memory tells me it was the amazingly intelligent comedian Steven Wright. What matters is what this person said. He looked straight into the camera and remarked, "Sometimes I look at life like this," and then he turned his head sideways. The message was simple. Look at things from a different point of view once in a while.

Such a simple message, but that brief moment was so powerful to me and was a quintessential building block for me becoming a musician.

It's assumed that musicians, like most artists, view the world in a different way. I certainly live up to that notion. Both of my parents were pretty straightforward, and no one in my family seems to be an abstract thinker, and yet I live my life completely outside the box. I don't think it's hereditary. The memory above is one of many examples to come where a thirty-second viewpoint from a complete stranger clearly defined part of who I have become.

I recall that moment almost every single day. I remember how excited I got as I thought, "Yeah, yeah, I get it. Look at life differently." It was genius to me. If it was Steven Wright, then Steven, you're like Einstein to me. Thank you so much.

I have always had a great interest in why anyone does what they do, and how we were molded into who we are.

For the mere sake of conversation and trying to connect on a deeper level of understanding during the apologizing phase of the end of my marriage, I would often say, "I'm sorry I did this, but I think I did it because . . ."

Generally, people are conditioned to blame others for their mistakes, and it may have seemed like that was what I was doing by trying to explain my actions. But in the end, I was just searching and finding out what made my marriage fail.

My wife's perception—there's that magic word again—was, and still is, totally different. The more I tried to convince her that I was not passing the blame, the angrier she got. I'd hate to say I eventually gave up on trying to make her understand my point of view—that's not in my nature—but I came to realize that we simply weren't able to get on the same page on this topic. So I put it away in the hope of not letting it go, but keeping it tucked away until one day when we could be on the same page again.

My mother passed away when I was only twenty-five. She took with her any and all information about her and her family. My family tree on her side is like the near-lifeless pine tree in the old Charlie Brown Christmas special. I don't know what illness ran in her family. I don't know if we had any heroes or villains. I know nothing. It was her passing that kicked my interest into action and led me on a huge journey to learn, instead of wondering what makes people tick. For the better part of fifteen years, I've learned a lot about people while trying to unlock the mysteries of my mother, Patricia Evick.

All those years of searching certainly gave me wisdom and insight, but what about my own proclaimed flawless little self? After all, in the end we are left with only ourselves. Shouldn't I be the mystery I'm trying to solve, not my dead mother or the mother of my children? My mistake was worrying about other people and their quirks.

My separation changed all that. It opened my eyes to what the real focus should be, and has been the inspiration that has led me down this retrospective journey through my own life.

In hindsight, the break-up showed me clearly that this once extremely resilient child, who believed his youth was perfect as it was happening, was being molded into one strange and almost dysfunctional adult. I thank God every day that I've been granted refuge in the land of rock and roll because I'm one hundred percent certain I couldn't function in the real world.

Chapter Two
It Didn't Even Happen To Me

Probably the single most powerful story that has haunted me for as long as I can remember is of the day my father chose to break up his first family. That happened years before I was born. My father had caught his wife, *not my mother*, having an affair, which is obviously not uncommon; neither is choosing divorce in that situation. However, it's what follows that still haunts me.

The story goes like this: my father packed his car and, without warning to my soon to be brothers and sister, headed out of town. As he drove away, he saw my oldest brother who was still a child himself playing on the street corner. He slowed down, leaned out the window, and said, "Son, you're the man of the house now." Then he simply drove off.

Stop and imagine what pressure that puts on a

child. Any young boy dreams of being a man, and all kids love their mother like a soldier loves their country. Obviously, my brother took his new title and did all he could with it.

Those eight words, "Son, you're the man of the house now," though they were not spoken to me, were instrumental in who I have become, and they were spoken more than a year before I was born.

While this is about what effect those words had on me, the flip side is that my oldest brother is well into his fifties, has three children of his own, and many grandchildren. His marriage, like most others, has endured its share of turmoil and tragedy, but he stood proud, as did his wife, with a single goal: that through thick and thin they committed to raise a family together and they would succeed. While I wasn't as successful as him and his wife, their influence and inspiration certainly kept me in the fight longer than most men I know.

What my dad did to my brother still resides in the darkest parts of my heart and mind, where anger and hate live and stew no matter how hard I try to suppress them. The anger I carried for my dad was not from his choice to divorce his first wife, but the way he delivered the information to my brother.

I guess I have to one day come to terms with the fact that if this event had not happened, then my dad would not have married my mother. I wouldn't be here to be mad about it today, so I should be strangely grateful. I'd have never been born had there been a different turn of events.

Even before I had kids of my own, I pondered how any man could just walk away from his children. For most of my childhood, my brothers and sister from my dads previous marriage were kept at quite a distance from me, and despite the fact that their mother had had an affair, they seemed to favor her, probably for the simple fact that she stayed. I must add that after years of not knowing the whole story, I have now been led to believe my dad wasn't as innocent in all this as I may have thought. He knew my mom before he left his first wife, if you get where I'm going.

I certainly believe in the power of staying. My friend Chuck has always stayed by me. He's the drummer in my band. We owned a business together before we were in our twenties, made music together, and have toured the world together. People consider him to be a pretty unemotional and somewhat selfish human being. We have had more arguments and fistfights than any two people I know. We don't have a lot in common, and if we met for the first time today we would probably hate each other. But many times now when I'm feeling depressed, I make the joke that in the last thirty years the only one who stayed was Chuck, and for that alone he is forever etched in my history as one of the best friends, if not *the* best, I have on the planet.

That isn't the only reason though. He has endorsed some of my craziest plans and schemes, followed me into poverty and debt, and came out the other side as one of the best and most well-known rock-and-roll drummers in the United States today. He's my rock-and-roll brother until the end, because he stayed. My point is simply, like my brothers' mother did, "staying" is probably the most powerful gift you can give someone. It brings with it an overwhelming amount of tolerance and forgiveness. In fact, oftentimes I wonder how I could ever repay Chuck for his time spent by my side.

I realize there are two sides to every story. I'm also sure there are a million other reasons I still don't know about that led to me not having relationships with my siblings; one being my incredibly strange and beautifully unique, yet overly protective and opinionated mother.

But this story is about what I do know, simplified down to the important facts and my perception of those facts, and how it affected me and eventually my own children.

Even though I had siblings from my father's first marriage, and occasionally they would even live with us for short stints, I grew up feeling like an only child. Many of my friends had brothers and sisters.

My friend Charlie, who lived a few doors down, came from a divorced family. His dad had remarried and had a couple of kids with the new wife, but they were a family. At an early age, I was introduced to, and well aware of, functioning broken families. I can't even explain the jealousy that made me feel. Although I never really thought of Charlie's stepmom as a stepmom at all, I do remember being fascinated when I heard him call her "Susan" instead of "Mom." I even tried to call my parents by their first names for a few minutes. They did not approve.

I would knock on Charlie's door after dinner when I was between the ages of five and ten. There were times when Charlie's stepmother would answer the door and say, "Sorry Pete, we are having family time."

I couldn't even comprehend what that meant. Sometimes Charlie and his older brother would have to do the dishes, and I would stand outside their window and watch. I was as jealous as any kid could be. You'd think they had their own Pac-Man machine and weren't letting me play, the way my heart felt. But to me what I saw was two brothers bonding. I'd have rather had that than all my Star Wars toys, and I had a lot back then.

I craved family, and almost with each passing

second my hate for my dad's actions grew. I blamed how he'd handled the situation for why technically I had family, but at the same time felt like I didn't.

Through my family's break up, I'm trying to forgive my dad. Even as my separation was happening, I made it very clear to my wife that my children would always know the truth.

My children's knowing the truth was my big stand. They would know I had begged her to stay and she chose not to. That was very selfish of me and without a doubt could have been handled with more love, caution, and care. But the impact of my father's actions was so huge that I couldn't bear for my kids to have the same feelings toward me as I had toward my dad.

It never occurred to me that they could possibly carry the same pain; only it would be toward their mother, not their father. What a crucial mistake. How could I be so heartless and outright stupid? I spent my life preparing to protect my children from my own pain, should the situation arise, but when it did, I managed to serve up the same kind of visions and memories that may eventually harden their hearts the way it did mine.

After I'd had children of my own, my sister-in-law repeatedly tried to explain to me that it was my job to break the cycle that my father had started. Maybe it was his father before him that started it. I'll never know because our family history on my mother and father's sides both seem to start and end with them.

While my sister-in-law and my oldest brother Mike, as well as my sister, Beta, and her husband were able to break the cycle in their families, I kept the fire burning. I only hope that I'm smart enough now to find the words and actions to make sure my kids don't carry any of this with them. It's certainly not their mother's fault. I was selfishly trying to protect my own image, a trait learned and required in the twisted world of rock and roll, where you're expected to be the bad boy, yet still need everyone to love you. It now seems that I channeled my inner publicist persona and may have framed my children's mother.

What only took a moment to hear, just eight words—*Son, you're the man of the house now*—led me on a silent and unchangeable path even though I'd only heard what happened after the fact and secondhand at that.

As a kid, I was normal, happy, well-adjusted, and all that, but I carried a dark brewing storm in my heart that only showed its ugly head more than thirty years later. There aren't enough apologies in the world to make it up to my children or their mother. The mere folklore of my family tree put this dent in my adult character and may have caused irreparable future damage to my family.

Chapter Three
The Chicken or the Egg

As a musician you are classified as an artist, and with that come labels like "strange" or "eccentric." Often social class dictates those labels. I've always said the only difference between eccentric and strange is the size of your bank account. Both words are often used to explain the awkwardness the *normal* feel when having to engage with the *weird*.

I have been accused of being both. So . . . my question resembles one of life's oldest questions: which came first, the chicken or the egg?

Only I wonder, is it being labeled an artist that makes us strange, or is it being strange that makes us an artist?

I have a vivid memory, not even tucked back a little; instead it sits in the forefront of my senses every morning when I wake up and every evening when I go to bed. While there are many moments that I describe as having defined my character, most are geared toward who I am emotionally. This particular memory, however, deals with what I consider the defining moment that carved the path to my career and what may become my legacy.

I was entering the fourth grade, and my friend Mike was in Cub Scouts. None of my other friends were in Scouts, except maybe Jim and Deron, but they didn't live on my block. I came from a neighborhood where we didn't really do those things; we didn't join sports teams or participate in school events. However, my nature was to be much more social than all my friends. Back then I was considered too talkative. I talked to everyone and anyone.

The Scouts would change all that.

I was very creative; I liked to build things, I liked to learn, and I loved to be around new people. I wanted to be in Cub Scouts like my buddy Mike. Whatever process it took, my mom did it, and I remember the excitement of going to the local department store to get my uniform and Scout guide. For weeks it was the only thing I thought about. I was going to be the best Cub Scout I could be.

I guess now's a good time to point out exactly how eager and innocent a child I was. Even at that young age, I had already been exposed to rock and roll, and was already in love with KISS and Van Halen. Years earlier I'd been sent home from kindergarten for drawing too many pictures of Gene Simmons, but I also wanted to get good grades, I wanted adult approval, and basically wanted to be one of the good kids.

The day before my first Cub Scout meeting, my friend Mike was walking home from school with me. Innocently, he shared something the den mother had told them at their last meeting.

She'd said, "Boys, we have a new Scout joining the group next week. His name is Pete, and he's a very strange kid."

Bam!

What was a little boy supposed to do with that information, and why on earth would she have said that to the other kids? Talk about giving the new kid a disadvantage. As far as Mike goes, many times through the years, while telling this story, I've been asked if Mike was just being cruel. The answer to that is no. Mike was the kindest kid in our neighborhood. He was raised with the most manners and values of any of us. He was just being an innocent kid telling his buddy what he had heard.

For the record, I have to say Mike is still one of my closest friends. He's a brother. His memory tells him that the den mother called me "special" not strange. Either way, I was not in any special education classes and ranked high in my class, it's obvious what she meant, and my brain heard it as "strange" and I've carried that all of these years.

I often try to figure out just what was so strange about me and how a woman who had never even met me came to that conclusion. Life was pretty simple in our small town; there really wasn't a ton of variation. I'm not sure any of us had the option of being too different from one another. Mike equaled me in my love of rock and roll—his parents had even taken him to see KISS in concert.

But like any outcast, I wonder now, was my reputation already preceding me?

Which takes me to the chicken-or-the-egg question—what comes first?

Was I born eccentric or did I grow into strange?

As an adult, I have great pride in being different. I take great satisfaction knowing I dance to the beat of my own drummer, and for better or worse, have always done it my way. To succeed in the entertainment business you, without a doubt, need to possess unique qualities. Perhaps I was born with them, and it being called to my attention at such an early age was just the ignition of the spark to lead me on my path. Maybe it was divine intervention, and hearing those words was some sort of verbal confirmation and approval to march forward and be weird.

In the end it's the part of me I'm most proud of, but it did not come without a cost. I've spent my life with an anxiety and fear of people that has truly been crippling. I rarely went to parties in high school unless I was performing at them, and suppressing the fear of walking into a room of people I don't know takes a series of mental exercises and preparation that are exhausting to me to this day.

I am convinced that everyone is laughing at me at all times. It's been thirty years, and there's not a therapist who can convince me differently. The struggle I've had meeting girlfriends' parents has been comical. Thank God I chose a career that doesn't involve going on job interviews. Going through drive-throughs alone is almost impossible, and even ordering pizza is a task. For the many years I was married, if I could convince my wife to place the order, I was a happy man. To me the most brilliant invention of our time is the Chipotle and Papa John's mobile apps. I can eat without interaction now. The age of the text message suits me perfectly. I can have a thriving social life without being near another person. Keep in mind though, it's not that I don't like people—I generally love everyone; I just think they all hate me.

Our band has been known to fly several times a week, and the guys all laugh but have become very understanding and helpful with my situation. They are always kind enough to go to the ticket counter for me if needed, usually taking my ID with them and having to point me out to the people working there. The funny thing is that my reclusive actions, given my job and success, are often perceived as arrogant rock-star moves.

If they only knew I was scared stiff like a deer in the headlights. Those closest to me know that if at all possible I like to be alone, and can sit in my basement in the dark for days, happily working on new music in my studio. In recent years, I have spent a lot of time on a huge ranch on the outskirts of Scottsdale, Arizona. I have gone weeks without leaving the property and days without seeing another person other than said ranch's owner, and it's been heaven to me.

For all you astrology types, the other half of the cocktail that fuels Pete Evick, the lemon to the lime and the yin to the yang, is that I'm the poster child for a Leo. I crave attention and affection. In fact, the Leo in me was probably the biggest part of my failed marriage. I craved more than my Gemini counterpart was willing to give. For all my social phobias, once you get me one on one, I'm a chatterbox and an open book to anyone willing to participate in conversation with me or just listen, for that matter. But make no mistake, I will never initiate anything, be it a simple hello or a passionate intimate exchange. I have to be one hundred percent certain I'm welcomed, invited, and wanted. Once that happens, though, the lion, the leader, and the alpha male in me come on strong.

I often wonder if the Leo in me would have been the life of the party, the class clown, or student body president had I never heard what the scout leader had said about me.

More times than not, people try to call bullshit on this whole part of me, because eventually I'm asked, "So then, do you get nervous when you go on stage, or on TV or the radio?"

My answer is and always has been no. I don't suffer from any sort of stage fright and never have. I believe the reason is this: when you're on stage and there are thousands of people watching you, even though your souls connect through the music, they still can't actually get to you. You're a king and you're untouchable, but it's deeper and much less arrogant than that sounds.

It's an honor. To be an artist is a gift, and to have the power to make people happy, or at least forget their everyday stress even for an hour, is a responsibility. If you have that gift, in my eyes you had better use it. If I know that I have someone's approval, then my fears are instantly erased. If you are at the show, you obviously came because you wanted to, and you obviously know I'm going to be there. When I walk onto the stage, it's not like I'm walking into a room and someone says, "Who invited him?"

When I'm performing, it's my party.

I'm supposed to be there, and that's a very safe

feeling. In the case of playing with iconic front man Bret Michaels, which I've done for a decade, it certainly is *his* party, but he's been so vocal and kind about telling his fans we are a band and friends, that they seem to have taken me in as well, so the same comfort of "supposed to be there" rings true. Bret didn't need to do that, and other people of his status do not treat their band like this. I'm forever thankful.

So there ya have it, the perfect recipe for a walking contradiction. Living, breathing irony at its finest—one part hurt child scarred from the ignorant words of a small-town Cub Scout den mother, one part megalomaniac, attention-starved Leo. As simple as a concoction of Jack and Coke, with the same sweet-yet-fiery result.

Intriguing combination, don't ya think? One day I should find that Cub Scout leader and thank her, I guess, because my fear of people provided me with a lot of extra practice time on that guitar.

Interestingly enough, while I paint this story with somewhat of a positive ending as far as my career goes, the father in me keeps the negative effects close to my heart and watches my children's every move with fear for their normalcy. A few years back, I was at a family event and one of my sisters-in-law was watching my oldest son, Gavin, play. I don't even remember what he was doing, but I remember her blurting out, "Gavin, you're so weird."

My reaction was physical. I jumped up like I was about to get in a fistfight. It was the same startling feeling you get at the end of a horror movie, when you're convinced the monster is dead, but in that last moment you see its hand move or eye open so the director can get one more scream out of you.

My initial thought was, "Oh God, here's the sequel—*Son of Evick: The Curse Continues.*"

I took a breath and let the moment pass. At the time my sister-in-law didn't have children and probably didn't think much of it; she had a smile on her face, and I'm certain there was no malicious intent. She has a child of her own now, and I'm sure she's more aware of the influence an adult's words have on kids.

I'm pretty sure Gavin didn't hear her, but it triggered a parental decision in me: to work hard on communicating to Gavin and Jacob that the differences in all humans are gifts that they should explore and exploit. But I've also been very honest with them about what is considered normal and accepted socially in our world, and the pros and cons that come from "fitting in."

For a few years, Gavin chose to grow his hair long, like mine. The overwhelming feeling that he notices, likes, and wants to be like me was a reward greater than anything I've known. While something as simple as a haircut is meaningless in the grand scheme of life, I've explained to him the jokes and jabs that come with this choice.

Remember the lyrics to the Bob Seger song, *Turn The Page*? You know the line about men having long hair and people asking is that a woman or a man?

I've watched my son experience these comments and jokes already, surprisingly from adults, who somehow found it acceptable to make said jokes to a ten-year-old boy and ask if he's a boy or a girl. But with pride I smiled because Gavin knew it was his choice. I watched him respond with confidence, "I'm a boy."

When I see the confidence on his face, I know that somehow I did what my parents didn't do for me; I've made Gavin happy and proud to be who he is. No den mother is going to break my son's spirit. He has since chosen to cut his hair, and that too was all up to him. I watched as he pondered it for weeks, maybe even months. It was quite fun to watch an innocent little boy make fashion-conscious decisions that maybe most children don't get to make. The amount of thought he put into it and him talking to me about the pros and cons was not only amusing, but also very fulfilling.

Coincidently, my younger son, Jacob, has decided to join Scouts. I was very excited for him yet cautious due to my history. I've joined him for several meetings and outings, and am happy to report his Scout leader is awesome, and Jacob seems to be enjoying it very much.

I'm one lucky dad.

Chapter Four
The Truth Does Not Always Set You Free

I was in fourth grade. I remember it like it was yesterday. I was sitting at my desk doing fractions, and everything was going great, until a girl I'd known since kindergarten came up to my desk.

In the sternest voice a ten-year-old could possibly have, she said, "Give me my ruler back."

What? The accusation confused me. "I don't have your ruler," I said, completely unaware of what was going on. I didn't take her ruler, and to this day I still can't figure out why she thought I would've stolen it.

Stealing? It just wasn't something I'd even thought about, and besides that, I had my own ruler, a white plastic one that I had some strange attachment to. I loved to put my pencil in the little hole in the center and spin it around like a propeller.

I didn't want or need her ruler, but no matter what I said in my own defense, this girl was not going to change her mind. She'd decided that I was the thief.

At least the teacher waited until after the school day to search my desk and my book bag instead of embarrassing me in front of the class. I wasn't afraid. I knew I hadn't taken the ruler, but I was saddened by the thought that someone could really believe that I'd do such a thing. The teacher said she believed I hadn't taken the ruler, but she still went through the motions of searching my desk and having me empty my book bag. I'm sure I looked numb as I stood there, knowing I was innocent.

I was crushed because I thought this girl and I were friends, and I couldn't understand how all this had happened. I wondered if someone had set me up.

I apologized to the girl over and over. Even though I didn't steal the ruler, I was sorry that someone had. I desperately wanted to solve the mystery.

The accusation broke our friendship, and I wanted our friendship back. In fourth grade your social life is pretty limited to the kids in your neighborhood. Where I grew up, everyone knew everyone.

It doesn't take a genius to imagine how horrible it feels to be the only one not invited to the birthday party in small-town America. I was already "the strange one" as labeled by the heartless den mother; now I was the thief? Not a chance. Even at ten years of age, self-preservation and image control are powerful things.

That girl never did apologize, and her ruler never was found.

Even writing about it now, I'm shaking my head wondering what happened.

I still live in the same town I grew up in, and although it's not a small town anymore, it can be a small world. About eight years ago, one of my friends started dating the girl who'd accused me of stealing her ruler in the fourth grade, and I ran into them at a party. As a thirtysomething-year-old adult, I think she was shocked when I approached her. Still consumed by the issue, I asked if I could speak to her for a minute. I explained to her that I had thought about the incident with the ruler almost every day, and that I needed to assure her that I never stole it. I actually wasn't too shocked by her answer but a little saddened by her lack of concern when she replied that she had no idea what I was talking about and that I was crazy to have worried all these years.

For a while we would see each other while she was dating my friend, but we never spoke about it again. She seemed almost annoyed by me reminding her of the situation and wanted it left thirty years in the past where she thought it belonged.

The funny thing is that I had been telling the truth for thirty-plus years, and while they say the truth will set you free, it did not at all. And even when faced with it thirty years later, I never really felt better, and the girl still never said, "I believe you." In fact, the truth has made me a prisoner in my own mind.

The positive side of this is that the already righteous do-gooder in me decided that day in the fourth grade that only if my family depended on it—not even myself, just my family—would I ever even consider stealing a penny. That's something that can never be taken away. It's an honor you can earn all by yourself. You don't need a diploma, you don't have to go through boot camp, and you don't have to go to church. It's one of the few things you can just be, and feel respectable about.

Now that says a lot for the world we live in, because it really shouldn't be an honor to be honest and trustworthy; it should just be what's expected of us. But more people than not are thieves—whether it's personal or intellectual property, the simple goodness of not stealing is more rare than seeing a falling star these days.

It reminds me of a hilarious skit I saw a few years ago from Chris Rock, where he's imitating someone who is proud that he got in trouble but only went to jail once, or got out on good behavior, I don't exactly remember. Chris Rock continues by saying, "You're not supposed to go to jail." Our society has really become accepting of the unacceptable these days. But I digress.

I'm proud to say I've worked for all I have, and believe me, the opportunity has been there to do wrong. The rock-and-roll business deals with a lot of cash, and I could have had my hands on a lot that I wasn't entitled to.

The negative side of this experience that far outweighs the positive in my eyes is that I developed this need to prove I'm honest. If for a second I believe that I'm being accused of something, I will stop at nothing to prove my innocence. It's like a calm determination comes over me to counter any doubt in my character. Something as simple as moving a remote control or eating the last cookie will cost me hours of my life as well as that of whoever accused me, not to mention any witnesses I may have to call to the stand.

To be honest, you don't even have to accuse me. You can just ask me, "Hey, did you eat that cookie?"

If I say no, the other person may just move on with their life. But in that moment, it's become my mission to find out who did in fact eat the last cookie. It's exhausting.

Over the years, who I am, the good and the bad, my character, has become all I have and all I care about. It's often like I'm starting my own personal monkhood where you give up worldly possessions.

While I still have nice things and live in our world, I have lost things and regained them enough to learn that nothing matters except who we are. I have taken that so seriously that it's truly an obsession.

I dream about what will be on my tombstone.

**Here lies PETE EVICK,
determined, hardworking,
paranoid, obsessive, and outspoken.**

To most, that might sound horrible to be known for, but to me, it seems great. It's who I am. I wrote a song once called "The Real Thing" and the lyrics to the chorus say:

*I always wear my heart on my sleeve
I always tell you things you can't believe
I am flesh, blood, rock and roll
Love and hate, heart and soul
I'm the real thing*

And that about sums it up. I am the real thing. Now

that I think about it, maybe what my tombstone should say is simply:

PETE EVICK
The Real Thing

Anyway, the simple point to this tragically long story is, in that moment in the fourth grade, I am certain being wrongfully accused of stealing that ruler created the now obsessively paranoid adult always out to prove himself an honest man and clear his name when it doesn't even need to be cleared.

On a somewhat comical side note, although this chapter is called "The Truth Does Not Always Set You Free," it could have also been called "The Thought Does Not Count."

You see, there was another lesson I learned the very next day about trying to be nice.

There I am, ten years old and devastated at the events that have unfolded. I wanted to make it right. I didn't have a dime to my name and I didn't have means of transportation, but I had my ever-creative mind and, at the time, a kind soul.

I went home that night with the day's events heavy on my mind. I got out my ruler, several sheets of construction paper, a pen, and some glue and went to work. I cut strips of paper exactly the size of my ruler and glued them together, one by one, until I had a thick, stiff stack. Then I carefully drew every mark of the twelve inches on the homemade ruler, including the half-inch and the quarter-inch marks. The way I remember it, this was an awesome and very artistic, yet functioning ruler made from pure love and concern. It's the thought that counts, right?

Even in the final seconds of walking up to give it to her the next day, I was sure that my gesture would be accepted as noble and sweet and all would be forgiven . . . Nope, not a chance.

When I handed my handiwork to her, she glared at me and said, "I don't want that piece of crap."

Those words hit hard. Not only the choice of words—I wasn't even allowed to say "crap" at that age—but because I'd been taught that it is the thought that counts.

I learned a harsh lesson that day. That the thought does not count. At least not to everyone.

Chapter Five
The Downside to Following the Rules

Somewhere in the journey from wide-eyed child to decadent rock and roller comes the moment in time where we feel so wronged by the right, so betrayed by those we are made to trust, that all regard for authority gets thrown out the window. For me, it was at the very unthreatening age of eight.

From the European angst of Johnny Rotten and the Sex Pistols screaming, "I wanna be anarchy" to the much more clean-cut, Midwestern, all-American John Mellencamp singing, "I fight authority, authority always wins" something, somewhere, somehow, always inspires us as artists to try to cause some kind of uprising against authority figures, or at the very least to disobey and try to discredit them.

I imagine most of the time it starts in our teenage years during experimental periods of substance abuse and/or rebelling against rules set by our parents that seem absurd and suppressive. In my self-proclaimed one-of-a-kind story, my lack of trust and dislike for authority-type figures started at age eight in the second grade at good ol' Loch Lomond Elementary School in my beloved hometown of Manassas, Virginia. The authoritative figure to blame was not a disgruntled cop, not a corrupt politician, not even an overprotective parent, but rather a seemingly quiet and sweet schoolteacher. Her name will remain anonymous partially because the thought of it still fills me with anger, and partly because I'm not gonna say nice things about her, so if she happens to still be alive and someone tells her about this, she may sue me.

This tale is deeply personal and has several disaster points within the initial plot. Looking back, it really seems odd that my eight-year-old mind felt all the things it did. Let's start with the fact that I wanted desperately to be the good kid, as I've already explained in other chapters. I wanted to follow the rules and be as squeaky clean as I could while still listening to rock and roll, even if it meant total humiliation. Like a soldier, I would die fighting for what I believed in.

This teacher's biggest rule was RAISE YOUR HAND. Do not get out of your seat under any circumstances, do not speak unless called on, and if you need something, again you must RAISE YOUR

HAND and wait to be called on.

Wanting to be the good kid, I took that rule to heart.

So, I'm sitting in class and the common urge of any human to have to use the bathroom comes over me. I raise my hand.

You all see where this is going, don't you?

Five minutes goes by.

The teacher sees me, but she chooses not to call on me. Ten minutes, the same thing. Fifteen minutes. I'm shaking and almost crying. The whole class is looking at me, and yet the teacher still won't call on me. Regardless of the obvious embarrassment about to ensue, in my mind just the feeling of all of my classmates' eyes on me, watching me be ignored, was humiliating. Eventually the unavoidable happens. I find myself sitting in a pool of my own urine, watching it stream down to the black-tile floor and along the other desks in my row.

I put my hand down.

I don't cry.

I don't do anything.

I look down and go back to my schoolwork until another student takes notice of the puddle and blurts out that I had wet my pants.

Suddenly, the teacher comes running over. I have her attention now. She actually seems mad that I've interrupted what she's doing. She acts like it's my fault. For the most part the class finds this funny, and I try to protect myself by just denying I had done such a babyish thing. A female student stood up for me, saying, "It's only water." As if to suggest that my thermos had leaked from my lunch box or something. I'll never forget the feeling of her having my back. To this day, it's rare to feel like someone really does have your back, but this little girl did. Maybe it had happened to her at some point. Her motivation is something I'll never know, but for whatever reason, her level of understanding was deep enough for her to defend and protect me.

I was rushed to the office and my mother was called. When she arrived, the ever-protective and overreactive woman that she was, she went off. You would think she was going to have the teacher's head on a platter.

In my strange innocence, my heart was pounding and I suddenly felt compassion for the teacher. I was sorry that she was getting the verbal beating my mom was delivering. I remember the fear that if she had ever liked me at all, she certainly wouldn't now. Despite the humiliation of my classmates' laughter, my biggest pain at that moment was disappointing my teacher. What had I done wrong that she did not call on me? She had looked right at me, yet not responded. Maybe the trauma of the event has erased parts of those moments in the school office forever, because I have no memory of the teacher's reaction to my mother's verbal assault. I don't know if she ever apologized or gave my mother any explanation.

What I do know is this: whatever my mom and the teacher said, they did not say anything along the likes of "next time, just get up and go." I know that, because that was the pass I was waiting for, and it never came. So while my mom probably threatened the teacher with her life, the topic of how to keep it from happening again was never relayed to me. Perhaps it was just assumed.

Life goes on, and for the most part, after about a week, the jokes stopped and everything was back to normal. At this point all my respect for the rules and my teacher were still intact but . . . at some point later in the year, it all happened again. Can you believe it?

I raised my hand. I waited. She looked, but did not acknowledge me. I shook. I squirmed. I peed, and the class laughed, but this time the teacher lashed out at the class. Even more embarrassing to me was that my friends and classmates were now being yelled at for my mishap. The emotional beating I would give myself for that would prove to suck beyond belief.

I must have blanked out from the humiliation, because I don't remember anything after the initial minute or two after the incident.

But when Friday came and it was recess, I

noticed one of my still closest friends to this day, John, and another kid who lived on my block whom I didn't care for too much were both sitting on the sidewalk.

Having to sit on the sidewalk during recess meant you were in trouble. Ever so curious, I went over and asked what they were in trouble for. John just ignored me, but I could tell he was angry. The other kid blurted out, "Because we laughed at you wetting your pants."

Wow! I had no idea. That incident had happened days before. Why didn't John tell me? Was he embarrassed that he got in trouble? Did he not want me to know he had laughed at me? Best friends let each other in on such things. Either way, I suddenly felt guilt and sadness and that I should sit playtime out with them.

It turned out that not only did they have to sit on the sidewalk that day, but they had to handwrite the words to a book called *Happiness Is* and turn it in to the teacher. I don't remember the books content, but I remember it always being around in her class. She used it for this kind of punishment and also tried to push it on us as some kind of inspiration. Who knows, maybe she, or someone close to her, wrote the thing; all I know is that stupid book was always there.

This time, however, there was no sympathy or concern for the teacher, just pure hate and anger.

The feeling of betrayal for letting it happen again and, to add insult to injury, making my best buddy sit out recess, in turn making him mad at me—it was all too much.

Somewhere in those moments was the birth of my rock-and-roll defiance and, to be honest, the birth of loyalty to my friends.

It wouldn't be until I was in my thirties and the start of my friendship with rock-and-roll legend Bret Michaels that I'd come across loyalty that I felt matched mine. I'd never met someone so similar to me in my sense of what loyalty means, but I certainly carried the loyalty torch even when I felt I was the only one who did. That similarity defines our relationship, and is probably the reason I've been invited as his wingman on so many of his rock-and-roll adventures, which have also become amazing and special moments in my own life.

It's funny because, in this book, most of these moments are defined with words; there is a sentence or a statement that I use to mark the life-changing moment in each chapter. This particular story does not have that pinpointed audio bite. Just the feeling that came over me on the playground. Perhaps my friend John's silence is that audio bite.

I still ponder what my defiance is really all about. Was it the embarrassment of peeing my pants, or the feeling of John being punished because of it? All I know is the teacher was the authoritative figure and she handled it wrong. She upset my mom, my friends, and me. She was not to be trusted, and for that matter, neither were cops, doctors, politicians, or any kind of leader from here on out.

I must admit, this attitude, it has caused me some problems along the way. While I'm proud to say I've never become a thief or a criminal of any kind, I have challenged the police more than enough times in my life, and have never let anyone stop me from doing whatever I wanted to do or going where I wanted to go. I've been on driver's probation since my sixteenth birthday because defying the speed limit is the simplest way for a young redneck from a family of wrench- turning muscle-car drivers to show you he doesn't play by the rules. That's something I've yet to grow out of.

I'm known for saying exactly what's on my mind—at all times—unfiltered and at the second *I* want to say it, not when *you* want me to say it. The days of holding my hand up and waiting quietly for anything have passed.

These days I have good friends who occupy all these authoritative positions, and my anger has subsided. There are cops, doctors, politicians, even teachers whom I trust with my children's lives and mine, but it only took me thirty-plus years to get there—thanks, Mrs. Unnamed Teacher.

But what about the loyalty thing?

To this day I've never gotten over John having to copy the pages out of that book. No friend of mine will ever suffer for, or because of, me. Because of that incident, I've spent my life throwing myself on the sword so that those around me could have a better life.

One example that comes to mind is a party in high school. It was held in a hotel in the next county over from where I lived. At the time I had not started drinking, but all of my friends had. The party was busted. The cops gathered us all up and took us out to the street. One officer told us that he was going to pick one of us to represent all of us, and if the person he picked failed the sobriety test, we'd all be going to the drunk tank. I don't know that they could have legally done that to a bunch of minors, but it's what he said he was gonna do.

I quickly started acting as loud and crazy as I could. The cop picked me as the one who would determine everyone's fate that night. He didn't expect what he was going to find. If you'd seen the look on his face when I blew into that Breathalyzer and came up 100 percent sober, you'd still be laughing today.

I was a hero to my friends that night. Thank you again, Unnamed Teacher. And while that's not exactly a story of loyalty to one friend per se, it makes the point that at all cost none of my friends would have to copy *Happiness Is* again, or go to the drunk tank if I could help it.

I often wonder what it would have been like if I'd chosen a different path where I had a boss and a schedule. Would I be fired over and over for refusing to raise my hand and be called on, or whatever the equivalent of such things in the work force is? Thank God, I was bitten by the rock-and-roll bug and blessed by the music gods, so that I might never have to find out.

What I do know is that despite the humiliation and embarrassment of peeing my pants in second grade, that incident provided me with the tools to be a loyal friend, and to do what's right for me at all cost.

Those two weapons in your arsenal are far more important than anything else in the second-grade curriculum. I guarantee that.

Chapter Six
The End of the Innocence

The loss of a child's innocence is an inevitable thing. There is no way to stop it. It means something different to everyone, but it happens to all of us. To some it's the moment a child discovers violence, or the moment they discover sex, and to others it may be the moment they have their feelings hurt for the first time.

It's in that moment that the whole world looks different, oftentimes a little darker. It happens in a split second, without your permission. I consider myself lucky though because years later, in another split second, I basically got my innocence back.

I remember the exact moment: I lost my innocence in a department store in 1983 just days before I entered the sixth grade.

To others it may have appeared that I'd lost my innocence years earlier. I've said it before; rock and roll became part of who I am early in my life. I was wearing KISS T-shirts by kindergarten and playing KISS songs on my guitar in elementary school talent shows. But aside from my rock-and-roll exterior, I was still very connected to my mother. More so than most kids my age, I believe.

My dad, who passed away during the writing of this book, was a provider, but not much of a father in other categories. He worked his fingers to the bone, putting in long hours to provide his family with a place to live and food to eat. That taught me a work ethic that led to my reputation as one of the hardest-working people among my peers in the music business. But because my dad worked all of the time, my mother was left to handle my upbringing. Maybe it should come as no surprise that I was a mama's boy.

Don't get me wrong. I was no wimp. Fortunately for me, my mother was one hard-raised, tough-ass bitch. A swing-first, no-apologies, stand-your-ground, WWF-watching, Elvis Presley-loving boxing fan. So "mama's boy" didn't equal "wimp" in my world. My mom could have probably kicked most of the dads' asses and still had dinner on the table at 5:15 in her day. She kindly passed these tools and views on to me.

My mom and I spent a lot of time doing things together, like going to the mall. I used to love going to the toy store and the pet shop, and my mother

always made time for it. But this particular trip to
the mall was the annual school clothes-shopping
trip at the local Montgomery Ward. Back then, the
transition from fifth-grade elementary school to
sixth-grade middle school was a coming-of-age
type of thing. Sixth grade had organized sports and
school dances, and fashion started to matter.

It was the fall of 1983 and the neon sensation
was coming fast. Parachute pants had arrived, and
the decade was about nothing but image. I was
growing up smack in the middle of one of most
infamous fashion trends in American history.
Somehow my mom thought I'd fare well in the
popularity battle with the lack of cool clothing that
Montgomery Ward had to offer.

You're probably thinking you know where this
story is going. That it will end in a situation where
my mother and I fight about practical clothes versus
something I saw Duran Duran wearing on MTV.
Not at all. Read on.

What happened that day is much deeper. It still
saddens me today. As far as clothes went, we were
just weeks away from the unveiling of the "Jump"
video, which unleashed the new fashion trends of
Dave, Eddie, and the boys. That was the kind of
stuff you couldn't find at the mall, other than the
ever-popular glacier glasses that Mr. Roth seemed
to wear so much better than me.

But this isn't about the clothes. Instead, this tale

involves a popcorn stand that had been a huge part of my childhood, a "cool kid" whose name I can't even recall, and my unknowing mother.

On every trip to the mall, my mom treated me to a bag of the wonderful popcorn from the popcorn stand in Montgomery Ward. For years, I was that happy, innocent kid, enjoying my popcorn while my mom shopped the aisles. I imagine it's really easy to picture, but what's hard to explain is that this was a tradition that we shared. It was sort of a ritual, not much different than the summer evening stop at the ice cream truck that was synonymous with suburbia in the 80's. It's the stuff that makes for special memories.

As we headed to the popcorn stand that day, our paths crossed with the "cool kid." In that one breath, I felt different. As much as I wanted the popcorn, I didn't get it. I couldn't shake the thought that when school started, Mr. Cool Kid would tell everyone he'd seen me in the mall munching popcorn like a baby with my mom.

Funny thing is, on the inside I'd already pledged my allegiance to rock and roll. Behind the closed doors of my bedroom, I was Ace Frehley all day long, and due to my mom's WWF boot camp, I probably could've shut the kid up permanently if he'd ever challenged me. But that never occurred to me. It wasn't my style *yet*. Instead, it changed me. In that very second, everything that was pure and uninfluential was gone. At that time in my life even rock and roll was pure. I liked KISS because I liked them, and nobody was going to tell me Van Halen wasn't the coolest thing that ever happened to my ears. I had my own opinions and others had never swayed them. Until then.

Suddenly, what other people thought mattered. I regret letting that demon get his hands around me to this day. I wish I'd just innocently outgrown getting the popcorn, but that wasn't how it went down. My mom appeared to be a little shocked, and I've often wondered if she realized what was happening.

The kid walked right by us; for all I know he went to a cookie stand and chowed down on some warm, fresh chocolate chip treats.

Not getting that popcorn that day had a long-term effect. I became self-conscious of everything. I lived in a very poor part of town, but the way the county lines were drawn when middle school started, we were bused into a richer school district. This weird little Cub Scout began to feel weirder and weirder.

I'd let peer pressure deprive me of my childlike desires, but interestingly enough, I never caved into other peer pressures. Even though I was right in the middle of all the events that are associated with coming-of-age, I followed my own code of ethics. Alcohol and other things started showing up, and just like my popcorn, I'd have none of it. I began to resent those kids in school who gave the impression that they'd still get their popcorn, yet function in the popular crowd just fine.

To add insult to injury, I was an enormous *Star Wars* fan and am to this day. In fact, I might be the only person you'll find who won't say a bad word about the prequels. I loved them.

Sixth grade was in full swing. KISS posters covered my bedroom walls. I'd drawn Van Halen logos on just about anything that wouldn't move, and my record collection had grown with the addition of Def Leppard's *Pyromania* and Quiet Riot's *Metal Health*. However, one shelf in my room was still dedicated to my Star Wars toys. Every movie scene that I'd personally slaved so hard to re-create was on proud display.

Word got out that I played guitar, and to my surprise, some other kids did too. One weekend two guys from the super-cool crowd came over to my house to spend the night. While cliques weren't a big deal to me, it felt good that they wanted to come to my house and hang out. We had a great time until one of the kids pointed to the shelf and said, "You still have Star Wars toys?"

There was that feeling again. The same one that engulfed me with the popcorn situation, only I couldn't hide or cover this. All those Star Wars toys were right there in plain sight. I shifted the attention to my KISS posters, but in my mind I knew when they left I'd have to take the toys down. For a few years I abandoned my dedication to George Lucas and the world he created that I'd loved so much. What a terrible, terrible mistake. But it wouldn't last long.

In high school, about the time you could buy the VHS copies of the original trilogy, I threw myself full force back into the Star Wars universe. I never became a full-on comic book sci-fi nut, but by high school my popularity was based on rebellion and a lack of concern for being normal. Most musicians are known for the ability to express themselves without the boundaries of peer pressure. I was no different. I'd eventually become pretty cool for being the killer guitar player in the hip hard-rock band, who came to the party but didn't party, and who loved girls but would invite them over to watch *Star Wars*.

For years I couldn't shake the nagging question of why I didn't get popcorn that day. I really wanted it. When I'd make other choices for similar reasons over the years, in my mind I was that sixth grader in the mall all over again.

Years later, I opened a recording studio in my hometown and was employing a really popular local musician, who, by the way, has gone on to be pretty successful. At the time, he was part of the Goth scene, all decked out in jet black, sporting a bright-green Mohawk.

We went to lunch one day and in all his Goth gear and menacing image, he said, "I want dessert. Let's go get some ice cream."

It just didn't seem like the kind of thing for an up-and-coming Gothic superstar and local guitar hero-gone-business owner to do, but I agreed. And in that moment, at the age of twenty, life changed again. I recaptured that innocence. I was inspired to never deny myself any of my desires. And I was overwhelmed with the realization that while I was twenty and still young, I'd tried to grow up way too fast.

Suddenly and forever since, there have been no secrets about things I like, what I want, or what I expect. Complete freedom is an amazing feeling. To allow yourself to let go of all inhibitions is to lead yourself on a personal path of spirituality that can't be taught.

That attitude has led me to some extremes in my life, like dying my hair metallic blue and wearing silver shoes no matter what the occasion, but it has also allowed me to stick to my guns musically and never fake it, no matter what the passing trends of pop culture threw my way.

The moral of this story is to stick to your guns. While most of the stories I've shared are about one defining moment, this one clearly had two. The moment I hid part of myself from the world in the sixth grade, and the moment I broke out of my self-made prison and told the world "like it or not . . . this is me, popcorn and all."

I don't know how life would have been had I never felt the way I did about the popcorn that day. I may not have appreciated the feeling of freeing myself as I do now. But as an adult and a father, that experience is a constant reminder to let my kids know that at all cost, it's always best to be yourself. I have spent many evenings expressing this to my oldest son, Gavin, and look forward to teaching it to Jacob as he gets older. I sure hope they get it, and pass it on to their children.

There's nothing more rewarding than being honest with yourself.

When I stare into my children's innocent eyes and hear their pure voices and honest thoughts, I pray, "Please, please, don't take their innocence away before their time."

Chapter Seven
The Day after and the day after that and…

I grew up in the '80s when the nuclear threat was alive and well, but then again, it was alive and well for decades before and honestly thrives today. I guess the '80s were more about the Soviet communist threat, but the weapon of choice that instilled fear was the atomic bomb.

As I'm writing this, I ponder when the nuclear threat will truly be over. For a few years, maybe even through the entire '90s, we were kind of lead to believe it was over, but now you can't turn on the news without hearing about some country's nuclear program.

A horrible truth just hit me as I wrote that.

The nuclear threat will only be over when the next, bigger, more frightening weapon is unveiled and probably used. After all, dropping the atomic bomb on the two cities in Japan was our introduction to the nuclear age, so why would it be different with the next big killing machine?

Try as we might, our society for as long as we can remember has been based on who has the bigger gun. I don't think that was how it was supposed to go for us humans, but it's how it went. Maybe we will be more peaceful creatures in the next stage of our evolution.

From the age of the caveman, history repeats itself. Spears give way to bow and arrows. Catapults, swords, and forged-steal weapons to guns, then automatic rifles. Tanks to weaponized aircraft, and then submarines to satellites with lasers.

Fear is only replaced by greater fear.

What does all of this have to do with me?

Well, I grew up in the '80s as I've said, and where most parents tried to shield their children from exposure to world crises, my parents didn't shelter me at all. In fact, I was always openly exposed to the world as seen through adult eyes and the evening news.

And it wasn't just war and politics. In my house, my parents didn't hide vulgar language or inappropriate TV; there was just no censorship. My parents smoked nonstop, and my dad, while never appearing as a drunk, certainly drank. My mom believed in violence as discipline in such a major way that she would without a doubt go to jail today if she were alive and raising children.

They say a child's brain is like a sponge. Sometimes I feel like mine was used to soak up dark and awful stuff.

In kindergarten I was diagnosed with an ulcer, and was told it was because I worried too much. As an elementary school student, I was more concerned with our world at war than art class, and I worried if God and Hell were real or if that was all fake, like the debunked Santa Claus in a chapter coming up.

I escaped with music. If it weren't for my KISS records, I might have died of fear and stress by the fifth grade. Let's be honest: my parents probably should have sheltered me from KISS. I'm still not sure why it was okay for their child to run around singing "You pull the trigger of my love gun" in front of their friends during holidays and birthdays, but for that, like so many other things, I should be grateful, I suppose.

It didn't stop there. I was always exposed to the news and clearly remember horrible destructive things like Lennon being shot, Reagan being shot, the space shuttle crash, all the hostage and missile crises, and stuff like that.

In the early '80s, as a sixth grader, I watched the movie *The Day After*. I clearly remember it being the first time I'd ever seen viewer discretion warnings. The network ran those warnings after every commercial break. But my parents didn't seem concerned. We watched the movie as a family. I understood what nuclear war was, and the media had imparted fear in me, like so many others at that time. But this movie did something different to me. The last five minutes shook me to the core, and it still resonates with me to this day.

My dad was a man's man—an auto mechanic, hunter, and all around ex-military tough guy. As distant as we were, his mere image instilled in me what men were supposed to be made of—never show fear or pain, and never cry.

But in that last scene of *The Day After*, an old man is standing in the nuclear waste of what was once his home. Another man with his family had set up camp in the rubble. The owner of the destroyed home approaches the new occupants and very aggressively says, "Get out of my home." The other man just stares at him, and then very kindly offers him a dirty old onion. He extended that onion as if it were a gourmet meal.

The homeowner walked away in what seemed to be disgust and anger, but then he fell to his knees in a total emotional breakdown.

It was so unexpected. Then the family man comes over and puts his arms around him in an embrace. No words were spoken, but I could feel the power of that scene. It was as if he were saying, "I'm so sorry we are camped out on what used to be your home, but we are all in this together and have *all* lost everything."

It was so powerful to me to see grown men like my father turn into crying, frail, weak beings that it left a lifelong impression on me. The idea that war can break a man, and nuclear destruction could break the world, just blew me away. I could taste that fear.

Since then, in my travels as a musician, I have met and befriended several Vietnam, Korean, and Gulf War veterans who are truly broken and doing the best that they can to function after being forced to see and be the things they had to be. War is so much bigger than which side wins. The individual parts of the giant machine are so fragile, so *human*, for lack of a better word. What lives on after the war cannot be considered winning by anyone.

Now don't get me wrong, I'm a staunch supporter of our military. Soldiers hold my respect at the highest level. But those images of the postapocalyptic wreckage from the movie stayed with me for a long, long time. The thought of war zones is one thing; you know, unoccupied jungles and deserts as Hollywood makes us believe. But when your backyard becomes the war zone and is destroyed, that's horrifying—especially to a child. I became consumed with the thought of society's destruction. It invaded my thoughts and dreams and that still concerns me. My ex called me a doomsayer, the type who thinks the sky is always falling. And it must have seemed that way to her, but I can tell you that every time I felt that fear, I envisioned the man from *The Day After* extending that onion. *How would I react in those circumstances? Could I survive that kind of thing? Would my family survive? If they did, would I be able to hunt and gather to support them? Would I be able to protect them?*

Thirty years later, all of this is now part of pop culture, with so many survival reality shows like *Doomsday Preppers*. It's good fun on TV, but in my mind as a kid, it was flat-out terrifying.

Many other nuclear apocalypse movies came out in that era, and I watched them all. One single moment in the movie *War Games* gave me my only pseudo comfort for many years. The scientist who invented the machine that was playing the war games had moved his home to a location right over a nuclear detonation spot. If the war ever became a reality, he explained, from there he would see a few seconds of beautiful white light and be vaporized instantly. To me, that sounded like the best option for dying I had heard yet. I was able to sleep a little better knowing that living just thirty miles from Washington, DC, must mean I would experience that quick death too. I'd never have to give or receive the dirty onion.

This nuclear war stuff led me down part of my musical journey too. Even though I was growing into a little metalhead, there was a song that caught my attention. That song was "99 Luftballons" by the German artist known as Nena. (In the American version, the song was "99 Red Balloons," but for some reason radio stations played the German version more often.)

It was an antiwar song, the '80s version of what music was all about in the '60s, and that struck a nerve with me. I listened to that song over and over again.

99 dreams I have had
In every one a red balloon.
It's all over and I'm standing pretty
In this dust that was a city.

The visions painted of our civilization in ruins were so clear I couldn't shake them, but I'd play the song over and over in my bedroom, even in the bathroom while I would shower, and I'd stare out the windows wondering, "Are the bombs on their way? Will I have a warning?" My middle-school years were filled with that worry. The edge wore off in high school, and maybe it was that I finally exhausted my brain a little with thoughts of global destruction, causing the anxiety to dull more as I entered into my adult life. Or maybe I just became less afraid to die, but the thoughts still haunted me.

At some point, though, my thoughts shifted.

Rather than fearing the possibility of being vaporized, I felt more of a curiosity. I had to figure out a way to survive it. I suddenly wanted to be the man with the onion.

Moving backward to the 5th grade, I'd been given a Commodore 64 computer for Christmas. The technology inspired me, and I dove in hard. I taught myself to program BASIC. I used my television as a monitor and I learned how to program graphics. My greatest accomplishment was an animation that I programed to play when you turned on the computer. The screen displayed a tree, a cloud, and a man, and then a missile soared across the sky, exploding into a mushroom cloud. Then came scrolling text that read NUCLEAR WAR WILL BE MAN'S WORST MISTAKE. I was really proud of the accomplishment, and the ability to share my message. I'd show it to people expecting some huge reaction to both my programing knowledge and concern for the world, but instead I got blank stares. While no one actually came out and said it, the message was clearly: "What is wrong with you, kid? Go play."

By the time I was in junior high, I'd expanded my love for Van Halen and KISS to include Quiet Riot, Def Leppard, and the legendary Ozzy Osbourne. As a guitar player, I was introduced to the sounds of his deceased guitar hero Randy Rhoads and the eternal rock anthem "Crazy Train," and have followed him since then, but in 1986 with his new and just as amazing guitar player Jake E. Lee, Ozzy released an album called *The Ultimate Sin*. The entire record was about the nuclear threat. He must have had the same thoughts and fears I did, and if a man that ate bat heads was afraid, it made sense that I was afraid too. The album cover had a mushroom cloud for the background, and in the foreground was Ozzy as some kind of giant bat monster and a woman with demon eyes. On this album was a song, "Thank God for the Bomb," which brought with it a new perspective. I owe Ozzy for giving me the power to sleep at night through these lyrics:

War is just another game,
Tailor made for the insane,
But make a threat of their annihilation,
And nobody wants to play.
If that's the only thing that keeps the peace,
Then thank God for the bomb.

For the first time, it made sense to me. There was no winning this kind of war. Pressing that button meant everyone dies. So why play? I had searched years for some comfort, for a reason to believe the war wasn't coming instead of why it was coming, and there it was in the second verse of a hard-rock song. Comfort. While I give KISS and

Van Halen credit for my musical success, Ozzy Osbourne is the grandfather of heavy metal, and that day I became a soldier in his army. Because of Ozzy, I could sleep at night finally believing that the presidents and world leaders didn't want to die, so none of us would.

I was finally safe from both the onion and being vaporized.

I remember sitting on the couch with my mom as I wrote the lyrics to "Thank God for the Bomb" in blue marker on a piece of lined school paper. I tried to talk to her about the lyrics as she half-listened, watching whatever sitcom was on. That was the first day I started feeling the drive to change the world, and I thought, why not start with my own parents. However, their concern for their TV shows was more important to them, so I quickly moved on.

It was all starting to make sense, my master plan.

Like Dylan, Lennon, and Ozzy, I would lead a revolution through music.

Maybe now is a good time to mention that, as long as I can remember, there's been a force pulling at me that says I can change the world. I have always felt like I was meant to make an impact. Back then, my love of music and my fear of the end of the world met face-to-face, and I started to believe none of it was by my own design. There was purpose assigned to me by a higher power, but I'd have to find my own way. As a parent myself now, if I'd been in my mom's shoes that night, I'd have been a little concerned but *Laverne and Shirley* must have been extra funny that night, because she didn't seem to be interested in what I had to say at all.

So, moving along, how did or does all this affect me in my adult life? Well, I'm still terrified of the end of the world. I still imagine it every day. I carry angst for world leaders and the thought that one egotistical old man can singularly decide ultimately if we live or die.

Years ago, a good friend of mine started covering "99 Luftballons" in bars with his band. He sang what I thought was the German version, and I asked him why he sang that, rather than the American lyrics. He said he wasn't singing the German version. He really didn't know the words at all, and was just making it up to be funny. I was offended. That he would devalue such an important message burned inside of me. I gave him an entire lesson on what the song meant. He looked at me like I was crazy, and maybe he was right, but those words mean something to me and I wondered how they didn't resonate with him.

Every time I turn on CNN, I fear the sky is falling, and now I worry for my kids' future. I do my best to make sure my children never feel as scared as I did. On the flip side, I learned a long time ago that there was nothing I could do about my feelings, so in turn that man and his onion developed my favorite side of me—the side that is pure rock and roll. The side that says, "The world may end right now, so throw caution to the wind and do what your heart desires."

My song "Spin" goes,

> *I can't guarantee that I'll be here tomorrow*
> *When I don't know what might happen today.*
> *I don't know why we're drowning in our sorrow,*
> *When every day is just another day.*

> *Chorus:*
> *The world keeps spinning round and round,*
> *without you, without me, without a sound.*

The lyric is inspired by the fact that no matter how hard I tried, I couldn't erase my thoughts and fears, but when you sit back and think about it, nothing really matters in the grand scheme of the world, because it goes on without us. We aren't in control. I started to live my life by this truth. I traded most people's everyday fears, like financial and social status, for that one fear of mine, and it has served me well. I do whatever I want when I want, without any fear of consequence, because you know, the sky might really be falling right this second, and I don't ever wanna wonder, *what if?*

I'm not a bad person. I don't do evil things. But I also don't let the fear of failure or being judged by my peers or authorities affect my actions or me. It's the essence of rock and roll. It's the way I live my life, and I may not have gotten to this place had I not had the fear of dying and total extinction etched in my brain more than thirty years ago.

That song, "Spin," was the song that finally landed me my first real record deal. That song turned me from a dreamer into a professional musician. So thank you, Onion Man. Thank you, Ozzy; thank you, Nena; thank you, world leaders; and I guess I owe a big thank-you to Albert Einstein.

During the recording of that first record with my band, Some Odd Reason, that featured the single "Spin," I also wrote a song called "To Whom It May Concern." The lyrics in the chorus are

I don't wanna change the world we live in,
I just can't go on like this anymore.
It's hard to find something to believe in,
When the headlines read and the TV screams of war.

The producer of the album, Richard Gottehrer, is an impressive guy. I was so fortunate to work with a talent of his caliber. Look him up. You'll be amazed at who he is and what he's done. Gottehrer has a career dating back to the '60s and has produced legends and written timeless songs. Anyway, we were talking about "To Whom It May Concern"; I'd written it in 1996, which by the way, is considered one of the most peaceful times in recent history.

I'll never forget Richard saying to me, "Pete, it's a great song, it really is. The problem is it's a war protest song, and there is no war to protest right now."

I remember thinking at that moment, just like I'm thinking right now, that the war never ends for me. That old man and his onion really got to me. He really got to me.

Chapter Eight
Accept Everything.....bet ya can't

Brace yourself, because this chapter is going to seem weird to most of you. I get that, but if you've stuck with me this far, maybe I won't lose you now.

I am infatuated with, and have been known to be consumed by, the possibility of alien abductions. Here's the absolute truth: I'm smart enough to understand that the mind plays tricks on us, and that a child who is sexually abused may turn that incident into what are called "screen memories" in the alien abduction world. Basically, that's when you take the horror of what happened to you in reality and manifest it as some totally different fantasy-like memory. While horrifying, this fantasy/memory—for example, the monster in the closet or the bogeyman—is easier for you to deal with than the thought of being abused.

I was never sexually abused. I'm certain of that.

But whatever it is that triggers the brain into creating alien-abduction memories has certainly happened to me. Real or not, I have perfectly placed memories, as clear to me as those of the births of my children, of being face-to-face with what is referred to in alien folklore as the Greys.

Here's the catch. If you've really had that experience, it's unlikely you'd run to the talk show circuit to tell the story, at least not right away and not for attention's sake. Maybe after you have exhausted all other thought processes and it's your last option in an internal fight for your own sanity. You are humiliated, violated, and feel like you have no control. To think something else can take you out of your world without you even being able to put up a fight is horrifying and belittling, and suddenly that "free will" that we are made to believe is the greatest human gift of all has just been stripped away, along with the fabric of the reality you've been fed since conception.

I believe that most people with memories like mine spend their life trying to prove it didn't happen, rather than brag to the world that they were taken advantage of by a 3-foot-tall, skinny grey creature. By the laws of physics, any adult human should be able to crush that little guy with one swift smackdown. Over the years, the only alternative conclusion I came up with is that I had a traumatic dental experience as a child. I hate going to the dentist to this day, but . . . think about it. In all of the publicly described abduction scenarios, there's vivid descriptions of the medical chair, the blinding light, the tools coming down from above you as if attached to wires leading into the ceiling. They are all much like things seen and used in a dental office. Even the mask over the dentist's face gives the illusion of having no mouth, which could explain the alien look. It's all the same technically.

So there's that. You still with me? I hope I haven't lost you, but this chapter is not about alien abduction and my magic moment in here isn't tied to getting a tooth pulled. All of that is for an entirely different book, if you're interested in hearing about it one day. But before I leave this thought, let me explain that when you spend your life trying to figure out how it *didn't* happen to you, eventually you have to say *what if*, and after that you finally, even if for a brief time, give up and commit to the conclusion that, *yes, it did happen*. That's when you go crazy. Your life stops, and you start researching everything you can possibly get your hands on. You stop at nothing, and that is exactly what I did. You can ask anyone who was in my life in my post-high-school years until about the age of twenty-five. It was so consuming that my musical career even took a backseat and some hard hits.

And now to my real point in this chapter: I've

always thought I was meant for a greater purpose. Many people who believe they are here to change the world believe that it was the Greys that gave them the information and the sense of purpose, that the Greys have chosen them to be the messengers of a greater consciousness. Some believe the Greys are our future selves that live in a world where humans are cloned and grown, and that because of science and evolution we have lost the ability to reproduce naturally, so they have returned from our future and are seeking to make noncloned beings and retrofit their society with the better parts of their past—us and our reproductive systems. Some believe the Greys are giving us warnings of how not to destroy our civilization.

Some believe, like I do, that if this is all real, then whatever it is, it must be part of a universal knowledge. It must be like one giant galactic peace summit that we aren't welcome to just yet due to our immaturity and negative tendencies, and they are trying to push us along in our evolution so that we get to the next level and can join the party in the stars.

Reality or not, I'm good either way. If I wasn't abducted, then great, all I had was a bad trip to the dentist more than three decades ago. That's a lot better than the tragedies life has thrown at some of my friends. And if I was abducted, then hell yeah, I'm totally down with the I've-been-chosen-to-change-the-world theory. I'm honored and accept the challenge. Here I come.

So, I'm in my early twenties and I have every single book you can read about aliens, UFOs, and the abduction phenomenon. This was all pre-Internet and pre-apocalyptic cable TV. Way before *Ancient Aliens* and *UFO Hunters* were the popular thing to watch on Friday nights for us antisocial types. This was real research. One of the coolest questions in all those books I devoured was the one that comes up among us doomsdayers. That question is: Upon first contact, will they be hostile?

Frank Drake, a radio astronomer in the late '50s and early '60s, developed an equation for probable life in the universe, known these days as simply the Drake Equation. It states that, if a species were able to develop technology to communicate and/or travel across the stars, they would have had to go through a similar technological evolution to our own. That means they would have passed the nuclear age and all other destructive developments and *not* destroyed themselves. Basically, it says if you are traveling the stars, you must have already advanced into the golden age of peace that we claim to strive for and you probably aren't going to show up with death rays. I personally would like to believe that. But who knows? I'm a *Star Wars* fanatic, and George Lucas clearly shows us that there is always going to be good versus evil in the

far reaches of the real *and* fantasy universe. Darth
Vader had a Death Star, not just a death ray.

I read and read and read, and at some point the
obsession, along with whichever conspiracy theory
you choose to believe, starts to mold your way of
life. Again, I chose the "I'm a chosen one" path.
That usually leads to the spiritual path of what is
most commonly now called New Age. While
considered far out there, it's not frowned upon by
the mainstream as much as Scientology. But like
anything else, there are bad eggs, like the whole
Heaven's Gate fiasco in 1997. For the record, I am
never going to drink the Kool-Aid, or ask anyone
else to, chosen one or not.

In my opinion, New Age is pretty much the
evolution of the '60s and the hippie generation,
with a little mysticism and science thrown in for
good measure. For the most part, it's built upon
peace, love, and happiness, but above all things it's
nonjudgmental. "To each their own" is a good way
to live and in all honesty should be the number-one
human rule no matter what god you pray to.

I digress. I've mentioned in the last chapter my
constant curiosity with war and peace. Eventually
that became a spiritual quest for me. If you're a fan
of peace, you stop worrying about the war, and
then wonder what part of being human make us
different than other species. What makes us turn on
our own kind? What makes us start wars? I can't

believe an opposable thumb turned us into warmongers; there's another piece to this puzzle we have yet to uncover about who we are and what makes us different than whales and monkeys.

For years I have pondered what the word "unconditional" really means. It is the single most powerful word I know, and yet I can't truly define it. I often ponder this concept. In the deserts of Africa, a lion eats a zebra. The zebra feels pain, and fights for its life, but not even upon that moment of attack does the zebra hate the lion. Not at all. You can see and feel it in the exchange of any species. Snakes and mice, or tigers and water buffalo—it doesn't matter. When you watch your innocent kitten eat a field mouse, he doesn't look up at you like he's happy that stupid mouse is dead. I believe that's best defined as unconditional. To sound cheesy and steal from Disney, those animals are accepting that they are part of the circle of life. Why are humans different?

Why do we get so mad?

Why do we get so jealous?

Why do we get so sad about things that are out of our control?

What went wrong?

So, back to those years as a teen when I was researching alien abductions, and reading everything I could get my hands on between customers at the mom-and-pop music store where I worked.

In one book there was a whole chapter about an actual discussion that was supposed to have taken place between an alien and a human during an abduction.

The human asks, "Why is it we are not allowed to join you in the stars? Why aren't we welcome to the information and knowledge of the universe?"

The alien responds, "You are still just children. Your species as a whole must learn to accept everything."

Accept everything? I read it once. I read it twice. I read it again. Then life changed. Seriously, my life changed.

My mind went to the lion and the zebra. This was it. I finally understood. It's about unconditional love. We, as humans, *don't* accept anything. We try to change every single aspect of ourselves and the world around us.

They say that the love between a parent and child is unconditional. I say that's total bullshit. Parents get angrier with their children than any other combination of people in a relationship. No matter if it's about grades in school, choice of image, their boyfriends and girlfriends, career paths or lack thereof. Even if a parent shows outward support, our species is laced with silent disappointment. It's humiliating on a galactic scale. As a whole, it appears that we are two-faced even to our own children.

Years later I wrote a song on my first EVICK record called "Unconditional." Much like the song "To Whom It May Concern," this was another war protest song, but this time it was written in the days following 9/11, and this time there was a reason to write it—we were at war.

I had to turn off the evening news
Convince myself that it ain't true
Every time I turn it on
Someone dies or something's wrong
Makes me wonder how
We ever came this far at all

So, do you think that you could be
Find the faith to just believe
Close your eyes and trust in me
And give yourself
Unconditionally

The moment I read those words, *accept everything,* I felt like I understood all I needed to ever know. I was on my journey to change our species from hateful opinionated flesh beings to joyful unconditional beings of light. I for a moment believed so strongly in the message just delivered to me, that I thought I'd change the entire world overnight. Without the Internet, before the term *going viral* even came to be, I thought I'd just tell a few people, and the lightbulb would go off in their head like it did mine, and by morning a bunch of alien craft would be waiting like school buses to usher us into our next stage of evolution. It wasn't quite that easy.

All day every day, to this very minute, *accept everything* flashes in my brain like a neon sign flashing OPEN in a local tavern. I believe it, and I try hard to live by those two words.

Accept everything.

I pray I see the day we evolve, even if it's just the next small step. But try as I might, I haven't been able to influence a change in our species, probably because I can't completely change myself.

The day of that realization, I walked out of the music store a changed kid. For all intents and purposes, my heart and soul did change that day, but not even an hour later the human in me was spitting mad at my girlfriend about something I can't even remember. I had already failed in accepting everything. The journey is hard. Why can't we remove that gene that is keeping us from being able to function unconditionally? Now there's a worthy scientific effort.

Before I got married, my fiancée only asked one thing of me: no more fistfights. (With other men, not her; we were not a violent couple.) I'd grown up a full-fledged white-trash redneck, and when I got angry, "hit first" was my motto. It might have been the only real lesson I think my dad tried to teach me; I talk about it in the next chapter.

I made that promise to stop fighting. Not only for her, but I hoped that it would keep me on my path to becoming totally unconditional. For the better part of ten years I kept that promise too. But every now and then my best friend, Chuck, or one of the other band members would make me lose my temper, and I'd revert to my old ways.

My intentions are good, but I still haven't made that leap. Why can't I shake that anger? Although I feel as if I'm 90 percent there, and personally proud that I've come that far, this commitment clearly requires 100 percent to call it a success.

Over the last five years, since Kristen and I split, I've really started to understand myself better and work hard to let everything go. I'm not to the point of *accept everything* just yet, but I've made progress. I'd say I'm at the "let it go" stage, and that's a step in the right direction. The reward of not getting mad, or not letting things you can't control get under your skin and hurt you, is much greater than whatever mess you're going to make in your fit of anger, and believe me, you make messes you don't even realize. It's the ripple effect.

Think about the ripple effect of a simple two-person argument. I'll even make it personal to paint this picture. Imagine that my lifelong friend Chuck and I get into a fight. We are both angry. We walk away in different directions, and two other people who may be in a great mood see one or both of us. They sense the mood. They ask, "What's wrong?" We both answer, "Nothing," but our body language is screaming something quite the opposite. They know we're lying. They are offended. They wonder what the hell is wrong with us, and leave wanting no part of that mood, but now their mood is a little tarnished. Then they see two other people. The first thing they say is, "Don't go looking for Pete or Chuck. Those two are in pissy moods," and then at least a tiny bit of the negative energy is passed on and the cycle continues.

Like the wake of a moving boat in the ocean, you are sending out negative waves to the world, and as far as I know there is no shore or breakers in our mental ocean. That stuff just bounces around forever. That's why our whole species needs to accept everything. If one of us gets off this rock and sends a ripple of human negativity into the universal party, it could be a real, real bad day.

I certainly don't have the answers to any of this, but this book is about my defining moments. That fraction of a second it took for me to comprehend those two words—*accept everything*—changed me. It spun my whole journey in a new direction that I'm certain I will be on for the rest of my life.

I'm confident that I'll eventually heal myself.

I will eventually evolve my soul.

I will eventually give off more good energy than bad. I hope I'm not too old to share how I achieved it with all of you once I figure it out. It might be through the lyrics of one of my songs, or maybe through a book like this.

Who knows? Maybe I'll have my own talk show about it one day. But until then, I challenge you to just try to love unconditionally, and see if you can accept everything. I bet you can't.

If you're anything like me though, this will test your brain for a lifetime. Even if you aren't on a journey of spiritual enlightenment yet, it will cross your mind once in a while. You will ask yourself:

Why am I mad?

Why do I care?

And maybe you'll find it in yourself to just let it go.

In fact, as cocky as it may sound, if you never had this kind of moment in your life before, I bet you just did. I bet if you were to sit down and write your version of this book, this chapter would be one of your life-changing moments. I can say that without ego, because it's not my thought or idea. I'm just the messenger, passing it on from a book I read about some alien's conversation with some abductee.

Now how powerful is that?

A book I can't even picture in my mind anymore, by an author I don't recall, and just two words. *Accept everything.* Those two little words have repeated over and over and over again in my head for more than twenty years. Wow, to me that's big.

Now, let's take this full circle. In the beginning I'm talking about my anger for being abducted and being robbed of my free will.

But the very beings that allegedly did this have lead me on a path of enlightenment and peace.

How do I forgive them? It's almost like a paradox. Well, interestingly enough, my other favorite word, other than *unconditional,* is *hypocrisy.* To all you who find it an act of war for a superior race to pull us from everything we know into an alien landscape and do whatever they want with us, I challenge you to consider the human scientists who pull sea creatures from the water into an atmosphere where they can't breathe, in the name of helping humanity. Or taking monkeys and apes from a jungle in the name of human medicine. How is that different from what these aliens might be doing to us?

The medical advancements gained from this practice are certainly huge and undeniable in our human perception, but those animals didn't give us their permission. So, are we not hypocrites to not accept a similar fate? With that thought in mind, I, like many other possible abductees, have submitted to the process we call alien abduction and welcome it for the betterment of us, them, or whoever it's helping. There's no riddle in there, nothing to ponder—just pure fact. Accept that.

Chapter Nine
Hit 'em First

My father and I weren't close. I loved him, and as an adult looking back, I'm sure he loved me too. Although I never really thought much of it growing up, because after all, kids are resilient, right?

Upon reflection, there weren't many life lessons that came from my dad. Even the "birds and the bees" talk was all of probably three minutes from start to finish. I can still remember that night clearly. It was right before dinner, and my mom was yelling at my dad about it being time to have this talk. He called for me to come to the dining room. When I got there, he asked me if I understood what happens between a man and a woman. I told him yes and tried to run off, but he didn't let me off that easily. He asked me to explain it to him as I saw it. So I gave him a thirty-second rendition that was probably a bit off base, but apparently close enough for him to approve because with a laugh he responded, "That's about right." Then he sent me on my way.

I have to wonder, did he really just not care, or was it uncomfortable for him? I remember my dad closing his eyes when a love scene of any kind would come on TV. Maybe talking about stuff like that was out of his comfort zone. He'd had several children before me. Actions clearly speak louder than words. He knew what he was doing when it came to the birds and the bees, but I also think he left his first family before he'd had to give any of them *the talk*. So maybe with me it really was first-time jitters. Who knows? I never will.

That short conversation was truly the longest talk I can remember having with my father about anything that was supposed to be of any importance. He sure took his time teaching me how to make bullets for his black-powder guns, or how to change a drive shaft. He spent hours teaching me mechanic-type duties so that I could help him out in the backyard while he worked on his friend's cars. Let me be clear, though: that was all side work he was paid to do so he could support my mom and me. I'm not complaining. I'm grateful for the work ethic he demonstrated. What I learned in his silence were probably some of the most valuable lessons he had to share. There wasn't any ball throwing or bike riding, not even any of the basic stuff. For example, I was never given any hygiene lessons from my mother or father other than to brush my teeth. The teenage stuff like deodorant and shaving all came from watching and learning lessons among my friends.

However, this chapter is about the one lesson he did give me, and it's the complete opposite of what every other kid I've ever met received.

My father said, "Son, if you think you're about to be in a fight, if you think someone's gonna hit you—you hit them first."

He basically gave me permission to kick anyone's ass I wanted. All I had to say was that I'd felt threatened, and I'd have his support. That's an invaluable pass to a white-trash redneck kid living in Manassas, Virginia, in the early '80s.

I grew up in a neighborhood full of boys. It wasn't uncommon for us to rally in a circle in someone's yard in a big act-tough moment with the kids cheering for us to "ready, set, fight!"

When I was in the first or second grade, my friend John was the toughest kid on the block. Good thing we were allies. He was the first friend I ever had. I remember watching him get into fights. One in particular sticks in my mind, where he took the other kid's face and dragged it across a chain-link fence like the fence was a cheese grater. Horrifying, but cool at the same time. With my new free pass to fight from my dad, John and I would be a team. I would be just as tough as him. Well, maybe not, but

I could sure be Robin to his Batman.

While some of this was harmless, and our young scuffles with kids on the block usually ended with us all playing together by the end of the day, the future wasn't as innocent.

By the time I entered high school, the fights had gotten worse. The kids got bigger, and the consequences became more frightening. Fights were no longer about name calling on the way to school. The stakes were higher: usually about a girl, or your girlfriend cheating on you, you cheating on her, or even worse—you and your girl could have actually broken up without the cheating, be on good terms, and the new boyfriend wanted to fight you just because you'd been there first. Young male ego stuff. There'd be a bunch of "he said, she said," some mental anguish, and then the huge audience would gather, anxious to see which guy would suffer severe embarrassment.

As I said, the kids got bigger, but I was blessed with speed. Armed with my hit-first attitude and stealthy punching skills, I was in and out before they knew what hit them. The problem was no girl really wants to see a guy fight. If you lose, you're a wimp. If you beat someone's ass, you're a bully. Your best bet was to not fight at all, but armed with Dad's advice I wasn't doing much walking away, so winning the fight was all that was left. But in high school there was a new consequence: suspension, or even worse—expulsion.

I liked to get good grades, and I liked to impress the adults. This new pattern of fighting didn't help on either one of those fronts. Suspension meant you got zeroes for your work while you were out. You didn't get to make that work up and you basically failed that grading period. That had long-term consequences that weren't easy to recover from, especially when you were proud of your good grades. I'd never missed a single day of school in my life, and I wasn't willing to lose my perfect attendance achievement. So I took my punishment through Saturday suspension. The name pretty much says it all. You had to go into school on Saturdays and waste your day. I guess that's what that movie *The Breakfast Club* was all about. I'll tell you this—it wasn't nearly as fun as it seemed in that movie. I hated it.

My dad had given me that free pass, so I hit anyone I felt threatened by, and I wasn't keen enough to realize just how stupid the cycle was. My mom, as I've explained in other chapters, was an extremely violent woman. I got beatings for having bad grades. I got beatings for not wanting to eat my dinner. I got beatings for whatever she wanted to beat me for. She was a huge WWF fan, and my earliest memories of TV are of Jimmy "Superfly" Snuka, and Andre the Giant. She was a born fighter. I have a vivid memory of coming home from school to witness my mom and sister in such a huge fight that my mother threw the lid to her record player (yes, it was the '70s and it was a record player) right at my sister's head. The cops showed up, and a neighbor took me to her house until it was all settled.

My dad, however, only hit me maybe once or twice in his whole life, and when he did, my mom would go nuts on him. That never made any sense to me, because she never hesitated to hit me. I still find myself shaking my head as I think of it now. I remember one night being in my room crying after my dad hit me. Listening to them fight was worse than the beating. The word *divorce* was thrown at my dad like a weapon. I decided that I'd run away so their marriage wouldn't break up. I jumped out my bedroom window, but they must have heard me because they met me in the front yard. Side by side, they'd somehow rebonded in a united front against the common enemy—me. Honestly, that suited me fine, and maybe that's where my strong conviction against divorce came from.

Away from home, back in the schoolyard, I'm not sure that I ever got a full-on ass beating in those brawls, but I didn't walk away from all my tiffs untouched either. I wasn't the tough guy in school; that wasn't it at all. I was small enough to be picked on a lot, but I held my own. Even if I wasn't the proclaimed winner of a fight, I was never the loser, if that makes sense, and I never had to battle the same person twice.

There was one fight, though, that I got through by the grace of God. Just out of high school, my best friend, Chuck, and another friend named Paul, who goes by the nickname "Bear," and I had decided to open a recording studio in town. We needed an electrician, and my dad recommended one. Although the guy was my dad's friend, he was my age. He showed up and the guy was big. We're talking 6-foot-4, maybe bigger, built like a Marine, and cocky. You know the type. We worked side by side on the studio each night, and each night he got on everyone's last nerve—I mean to the point where we wanted to kill the guy. But he was my dad's friend so we all tolerated him.

Until one night enough was enough. He stood in the open door of his pickup truck. He was so big that he filled up the whole space as he leaned into the corner of the door, with his one hand on the top and the other resting on the roof of the truck— almost the way a boxer would rest his hands on the top rope when he's in the corner.

This guy starts mouthing off about my dad, who again was the only reason he even had this gig. He thought he was being funny, but none of us found the humor in it. Mind you, I'm 5-foot-8, and that's with shoes on, so I was easily outsized, but I was getting madder and madder, until finally, like a spring, I flew up and knocked this guy in his jaw as hard as I could. I hit him so hard that the impact bent the truck door hinge he was leaning against.

Don't be too impressed.

All he uttered was a simple *ouch* before he came at me. I thought I'd met my match, and I was about to learn my lesson. As I scrambled for safety, I lost my balance and fell to the ground just as his enormous fist came to my face. At that very moment, I heard a loud crack. Like Superman, Bear had flown through the air and smacked this guy in the head with an unopened glass bottle.

As in every horror flick, the bad guy just gave a whiny *ouch* as he scratched his head. It appeared that he was prepared to continue the fight. To our surprise, though, he paused, took a look at the four of us (my friend Bart had joined us that evening), and must have realized it was a better idea to leave.

I should have learned my lesson that night, but instead I walked away with my ego inflated that I'd had the balls to hit a guy so hard that I'd bent his car door. Probably an even bigger ego boost was that I walked away knowing I had friends who cared enough to have my back. See, a guy can truly twist a story just about any way needed to make it work for himself. I should have just been grateful I'd survived. Instead the ever-present ego of the Leo in me turned it all around.

This fighting was a pattern that followed me to

the time I got married. My wife's only request was to can the fighting. Even though I'd figured it out long ago, she constantly reminded me that women don't think fighting is sexy or cool at all. I think what women really want is someone confident enough to not back down if it comes to it, but they hope it never ends up in a real brawl. I was happy to oblige. I was on the path to a more peaceful life anyway, so why not? For the most part, this was an easy request. I think I'd been looking for a reason to not be *that* guy any longer anyways, and love can make you do, and *not* do, lots of things you never imagined.

As the years went by, however, I started to believe—not that it was true—that my wife's sacrifices didn't equal my sacrifices and changes for the marriage, and bitterness set in. I'd made so many changes to fit into her world, and she'd not strayed from her path one bit. With this realization, I made the subconscious decision to get back to the "old me."

As I started to tear down the walls of the new me, my temper rose again. Most often that came out under liquor-induced situations with my, band members in EVICK. My marriage was failing, and I didn't like it. During this dark time in my life, I confronted everyone. Everyone was the enemy. Everyone was standing in my way.

My first real successful band, Some Odd

Reason, had just disbanded, and I was back to playing cover songs with my new band to pay the bills. I felt backed into a corner. In my mind, the world was against me, and that old lesson from Dad replayed in my head: come out swinging. But now I'd learned a new way to fight and that "hit 'em first" didn't have to be taken literally. I became a verbal knife thrower with cunning aim, and a razor tongue like no other. I'd make sure people would rather receive a physical beating from Mike Tyson than my brutal tongue-lashing. I was angry and I took enormous misplaced pride in this newly acquired skill. I was gonna beat the world one way or the other—physically, verbally, or mentally.

I look back on this era and can't even comprehend why any of these people still talk to me, but most of them I now call my closest friends. I've definitely been blessed. It's hard to truly want to make people happy and believe that is your true purpose, and at the same time feel like those same people, friends and family, actually hate you and are against you; yet that was the internal battle I was fighting. But in that dark time there was a ray of shining light in my personal apocalypse. A new reason to live. My first son, Gavin, was born.

Becoming a father instantly filled me with thoughts of all the things I would teach him. The first thing on my mind was to teach him not to hit. He wouldn't get the same lesson I'd received. There would be no violence introduced to this perfect little boy. My wife and I rarely fought. In the entire course of our marriage we only argued maybe two or three times. At the end of it, though, I'll admit that it felt like she'd become the enemy and all the respect I'd tried to pay her through the years was erased. I was verbally abusive. I was physically threatening, and the kids saw it a few times. Not all the time, but enough that I can never forgive myself. I never hit her, never did any of that, just bucked up like an idiot playing the tough guy. How do I erase that from my children's innocent minds?

The problem was twofold. First of all, violence was the one thing I'd vowed not to introduce, and second, this was not how to treat a woman. My dad never taught me a thing in that arena.

Not to open a car door.

Not how to be kind.

Not to pull a chair out.

Not how to dance or, for that matter, when to go in for that first kiss.

Nothing except that three-minute birds and bees conversation, although he seemed to have respect for women. He rarely cursed in front of them and always seemed to be on his best behavior, almost flirtatious at all times to all women. In fact, I'm sure most women found him to be somewhat charming. I didn't want my boys to lack those lessons. I've come to believe, especially after my failed marriage, that teaching my boys how to respect and treat women is the single most important life lesson I need to pass on to them, but I realize that I need to make sure I get it right as well. I'm a work in progress, but I'm sharing as I learn.

From day one, I instilled no fighting, no hitting, and I even tried no yelling, and that worked out pretty well when it was just Gavin. He was as peaceful as they come. I didn't think much about the impact of movies and games, though—so many are laced with violent undertones. Even my beloved *Star Wars* that I so innocently forced upon my own children's lives is the story of war on a galactic scale. Happy ending or not, it's war, and that's violent.

Jacob was born four years later, and it was fun, yet scary, to watch the children of a red-blooded white alpha male almost instantly compete for dominance.

As Jacob got older, and the fighting began, I preached the lessons. No violence. No hitting. No yelling, although I admit that I can't control my own yelling. It's just too hard for me to suppress it. I have a loud voice anyway, and sometimes they think I'm yelling and I'm actually not. I have yelled at my kids, but not with that razor tongue. I never throw hurtful words; just scream at them to stop fighting. I'm more mindful now than I've ever been, but I'll continue to yell while I try to keep the peace.

It's just the nature of my beast.

It's a vicious circle, and maybe some of it is just part of being male. They fight, and I preach, and they fight and I beg them not to. As they get older, it gets worse. Even as I'm writing this, I had to stop and go break up one of their scuffles. Interestingly enough, Jacob is four years younger and half Gavin's size, yet that boy not only holds his own, he comes out on top in most of these outbreaks. I've lived by the "you're gonna have to kill me to stop me" attitude when engaged in confrontation, and it appears my little Jacob feels the same way.

Almost every single night I ask them why they fight. They don't have an answer. I ask if they can try to be kinder to each other, and they say yes, but then it all starts again. Jacob clearly has the rage in him that my mother and I shared, and even though I've shielded him from the message my father gave me, it's like it's inherent in him. He will, without a doubt, hit first, with no remorse. Even though I punish him, he seems to have no regret. I guess in a way it's good. He clearly believes in himself; he thinks he's invincible.

Gavin is a different story. While he is a total instigator, he is way less violent, and always seems to look for a peaceful solution before physical confrontation. However, nine times out of ten, he pushes the buttons that eventually lead to the fighting in the first place.

I drive myself crazy wondering if when my dad told me to hit first it was somehow etched into the DNA that I passed along to my children. Maybe it was in my DNA all along and it didn't matter that he verbalized it. I never saw my dad hit anyone, but I'd heard the stories. I'd heard he was as badass as badass could be, with an uncontrollable temper and, like me, quicker than his adversaries. If he knew that, why did he give me the inspiration to carry it on? Why the free pass when he clearly had put it behind him in his later days? Not a day goes by that I don't hear his message replay in my head, and not a day goes by that I don't sense the urgency to undo what seems to be genetically wired in my children. Kristen and her family are peaceful to a fault. While I'm proud of my kids and grateful they seem to have many of my traits, I wish they'd taken the peace loving trait from there mothers blood line.

Interestingly enough, neither of my boys has been in any physical confrontations in school or during playtime with their friends. The aggression seems to be held exclusively for each other. Perhaps the school systems have found a way to filter it out. I know that bullying is the big buzzword these days. Stopping that behavior is the single most important mission in schools across the country it seems, and for that I am grateful.

My stomach turns thinking of my boys getting into the kind of confrontations I've been in. Even as the apparent victor in a fight, I have learned there is never a winner. Those battle scars are just too deep. I still carry guilt for hurting people over the years—from elementary school to the not-so-distant past.

After my marriage broke up, I lashed out at everyone who I thought supported or encouraged the breakup of our family. I was brutal. Even that, while not physically violent, was a very violent action. For years I was embarrassed. Eventually, I took a week and wrote apology letters and made apology phone calls to everyone I'd hurt in my whole life. Like in the television show *My Name Is Earl*, I tried to clear my karmic consciousness. I tried to shed the weight of my guilt in an attempt to free myself from my own mental hell.

I never want my children to get hurt or hurt anyone, but more than anything I don't want them to carry the kind of guilt I carry for such things. I so desperately want to protect them from the loss of sleep, loss of innocence, and the years of nightmares that come with hatefulness.

In my song "Unconditional," I'd written the following lyrics:

> *Oh I hate this hate*
> *It follows me*
> *It feeds on me*
> *Like a new disease*
> *And I can't run*

And I can't hide
It covers me
It makes me blind

Hate, anger, and fighting are powerful things. You get a taste, and just like Darth Vader you start your path down the dark side. George Lucas knew his shit. There is much more to his fantasy world than laser swords and spaceships. There are incredible life lessons in the holy trilogy. Now that I think about it, the first, and I think only, movie my dad took me to see was *Star Wars*. Maybe that's why we never talked. Maybe he thought I learned all I needed to that day, and maybe since that's about the only outing I can remember my dad and I going on, that is why I hold on to that movie with such fondness.

The interesting thing about teaching your children not to be violent is to learn to not fight fire with fire. When they're fighting, it's hard not to jerk one of them out of the mix, or at the very least to be physically intimidating, which is my natural instinct. Fear is not the best discipline, but it's a parents go-to reaction more times than not. After all, isn't religion really just our way of scaring ourselves into being good people? It's the same thing within the church of our family. It's just how we're wired. Scare everyone into doing what we want them to.

I used to wonder how someone like Ozzy Osbourne would be able to teach his children not to use drugs when that's who he was. Now I'm faced with nearly the same scenario, just replacing Ozzy's drugs with my violent nature. (Yep, I just compared myself to the grandfather of heavy metal. Poster child for Leos—at your service.

Moving to the present, I have once again found myself to be on the path of peace, and have been growing ever more nonviolent. I'm working hard on the *accept everything* concept, and with that comes the idea that there is no reason and no excuse for any violent behavior. That's no easy task, especially when your best friend and drummer is Chuck Fanslau (kidding, man), but I'm getting there.

I've made good progress. Now if I can just spend less time in airports with flight delays—a big part of my angst, but a necessary part of being a guitarist for a rock-and-roll legend—I should be able to completely extinguish the fire that burns within.

More importantly, I believe what will make it last this time is that unlike when I took a vow of peace for the sake of my marriage, this time I'm doing it solely for myself, because I want to be that person. I want to be better for *me*.

In the end, I think that's when we all find our road easier, no matter what habit or trait we are trying to break. When we truly want it for ourselves, everything is possible.

Now if I can get that through my kids' heads, things should be golden.

Chapter Ten
It's The Thought That Counts

In the introduction to this book, I talk about inspiring people to be their own mental archaeologist, to dig deeper into their brain than they ever thought possible.

When I wrote that introduction, the Leo in me showed arrogance: I assumed I'd already become a master of mental archaeology myself. I'd planned out all the chapters and was excited to tell all these stories about the *me* I had found through years behind this door, or under that stone.

In short, when I started to write this book, it was with the pretense that I was an expert on myself. However, just writing it has been an eye-opening exercise, making my brain work harder at cracking open mental rocks and finding new gems of turmoil and dysfunction that I never knew existed. Just like going to a gym makes your body stronger, my brain has been in overdrive, digging, searching, learning, and hopefully fixing some of my problems.

It occurred to me during this process that I have a serious issue that has affected me constantly in almost every relationship, romantic or platonic, that I have ever been in.

I hadn't intended to write about it, but now it seems like such an important story to share that I'd regret it if I didn't.

My issue is with the art of not only giving gifts but also receiving them. I am often complimented on my smile and how happy I appear on stage. I'm also often praised for my public gratitude for the career and life I have been given. But all that is done from the stage or behind the screen of my computer. When I'm performing, the stage is a sanctuary where I'm protected, and communicating via social media posts is easy when I'm sitting in a dark room away from the rest of the world. One-on-one, face-to-face, now that's a whole other story.

Those one-to-one interactions are different. Which brings me to the gift issue ... when presented with a gift of any sort, I become so nervous that I am nearly paralyzed.

My reaction is confusing to others. I've been asked why I didn't seem very excited, or worse, asked if I didn't like the gift.

This has happened so often that now when

anyone offers me a gift, I let them know up front that I get nervous about this kind of stuff, and ask if they'd mind if I take the gift and open it in private. Boy, do I get some odd looks about that.

Strangely enough, about ten years ago a unique situation happened. I was on tour in the Northeast with BMB. Bret and I both enjoy mountain bike riding. It's great exercise and a good way to get a look around the area we are in that day. A local bike company came down to the amphitheater with some bikes in the back of their truck. We were just going to use them for the day. Bret clearly saw how much I loved this particular bike, and right then and there, he bought it and said "Happy Birthday."

Bret had bought me this amazing mountain bike. That day I did show my excitement and gratitude like a normal human being. Maybe it was because I'd already seen the bike and liked it before he told me he was giving it to me. I didn't have time to worry about what the gift would be, or whether I would like it or act like I was supposed to.

I thought I was cured of my issues, but that was not the case.

On the inside, I'm incredibly grateful and overwhelmed every time anyone gives me anything. I receive gifts on the road a lot. Oftentimes people get my kids gifts too, and I don't care what it is, the idea that someone would even consider spending their time or money on me or my family truly blows my mind.

It's the thought that counts, and I truly believe that—despite my elementary-school ruler incident in chapter four. I'm pretty easy to buy trinket-type gifts for. If it says "Star Wars," "Van Halen," or "KISS" on it, I'm usually pretty excited. But still the problem remains. My face, known for its animated expressions of joy on stage, always falls short when it comes to the one-on-one. I'm left almost crying with gratitude inside, while a deer-in-the-headlights look shines on the outside. Maybe it's the anticipation of the surprise, the idea of opening a gift and thinking, *What if I don't like it?*

I've always been told that facial expressions speak louder than words, so I overcompensate and force myself to stay straight-faced, not because I don't want to look happy, but just in case for some strange reason I'm offended or appalled by whatever the gift is. It's almost like I'm playing a serious, life-threatening game of Don't Make Me Laugh. I'm also deathly afraid of the gag gift: this may sound silly, but what if I don't get that it's a joke? What if I think it's real and sincere—and even worse, what if I actually like it? That is overthinking at its finest, I know.

By the time I let my guard down, the moment has already passed, and I look like an unappreciative prick.

Ah, the misunderstood. (What a phrase—what

does it even mean? "He's just misunderstood." Has anyone ever been called "understood"?)

So, with this on my mind, I dug down deep to figure out when this reaction to gifts became part of who I am.

When I was young I reacted like any other kid. On Christmas and birthdays, with each gift, I'd yell and jump up and hug my parents—the whole nine yards. I have those memories. It did happen.

Then it came to me. I remembered the moment that made receiving gifts different for me.

I was already serious about guitar as early as seven or eight years old, and it was no secret to anyone in my extended family. The only band I knew about at that time was KISS, and that's all I wanted to know about.

I had a lot of KISS albums, but there were plenty I didn't have yet. I had just had my ninth birthday, and my aunt Gloria and uncle Jim, whom I loved to see, had come to the house with a birthday gift. I opened it with anticipation and excitement, and as I got far enough into it, I could tell it was an eight-track tape. Yep, I said that. I had several of those "high-tech" media-storage-type devices back in my youth.

As soon as I realized it was an eight-track tape, my adrenaline flowed in anticipation of which KISS album it would be. It had to be a KISS album. Why wouldn't it be? I mean really, they were the only band that mattered! Surely my mom or whoever would have given Aunt Gloria gift ideas would know this.

I ripped off that wrapping paper with excitement, only the cover didn't have fire, or blood, or rock stars in makeup, and there wasn't one sign of that undeniable orange and red KISS logo.

The cover had some guy who looked like he could be my neighbor on it, holding a guitar. It turned out to be Nils Lofgren, who is an incredible player and spent a lot of time in Bruce Springsteen's band. Later in life, I acquired an appreciation for him, but not at nine years old. This normal-looking guy was not in the KISS army.

I have no idea what my face said, but I do remember being vocal about not wanting or liking it. I also remember Aunt Gloria saying, "We know you're into that rock and roll now."

I'm smiling as I type this memory and think about how my Aunt Gloria may have come to purchase that tape.

I can see her strolling the record department of Montgomery Ward and saying to the salesman, "I have to buy a gift for a little boy who has taken an interest in the guitar and likes rock and roll. His mom says he likes a band called KISS."

The clerk escorts her over to the KISS albums. Her mouth drops open and her eyes bulge. I can imagine her being repulsed and totally against purchasing one of these for her nine-year-old nephew.

She probably pulled herself together and stammered out an excuse like, "I don't know which ones he already has. What other rock-and-roll music would a little boy like?"

The poor sales guy probably thought, "Look lady, the kid says he likes KISS, he likes KISS." That was about it for rock and roll in the kids' department unless you wanted *Chipmunk Punk*, an album of that day's modern rock hits performed by the Chipmunks, and yes, I did own that one too.

But for whatever reason, she ended up with Nils Lofgren, and in turn I ended up with a beating and a verbal assault from my mother that was so awful I'd suppressed it until I forced myself to confront this issue of why I freak upon gift getting. That's right, here comes the point of this all.

I clearly remember that moment now. After my aunt and uncle left, my mom gave me a spanking. My mother was very physical in her discipline techniques. It was her answer to everything. She screamed at me about how rude I'd been, how awful I'd made my aunt and uncle feel, and how ungrateful I was.

This is a real strange moment, because it's probably one of the most contradictive lessons a kid learns. It may very well be the moment in all innocent children that we are confronted with dishonesty.

Think about it.

Up until that situation on my birthday, I'd always been told to tell the truth at all cost. The truth will set you free.

But suddenly all of that changed. I was being beaten for not faking my excitement over a ten-dollar eight-track tape.

No wonder the world appears so fake and twisted. It apparently starts real early.

No wonder women fake their sexual pleasure.

No wonder men lie and say everything is all right when asked what's wrong by the woman who loves them, who happens to truly want to help.

From early on we are taught to fake our happiness, when the fact is, the intention of the gift giver is supposed to be making you happy.

So, let's get this straight. If they fail at pleasing you, you have to give them the false sense of satisfaction that they got it right?

Think about it, then think about it again.

Think about all the other aspects in life this bleeds into. I bet the lesson to act appreciative when receiving gifts is the moment in which we all become liars. I don't even think it matters if it's done through the Patricia Evick "beat you after you made the mistake" method, or through a preemptive warning speech made by a more peace-loving role model.

It seems the road to hell is paved with good intentions after all.

So, thank you, Nils Lofgren, for the spanking and the lesson in lying.

But I'm not done here. This is a two-part story. I'm not only dysfunctional at receiving gifts, I'm basically nonfunctional when it comes to giving them too.

Before I go on, I need to explain that I really do love and embrace the idea of giving. I would rather give than receive in all aspects of my life. I'd rather sing than be sung to. I'd rather cook than be cooked for, and so on and so on. I'm sure part of my problem is my ego, again pulling the Leo card.

I like to not only succeed, but be the best at anything I do. So gift giving becomes hard because there's no way to know what a person has received in their lifetime. It's not a real measurable thing, so the battle to give someone the best gift they've ever received becomes a wicked mind game for me. To make matters worse, when you're in a relationship and commit to the fact that you will be giving multiple gifts over the years to the same person, the stress of topping yourself year after year can really make you crazy.

There has to be more to what stalls me out though, considering that I'm an overachiever with the need to give. These concerns should only fuel my fire to be the best gift giver of all time.

But no. Instead, I choke. To the point where sometimes I avoid gift exchange completely with people for whom it should be commonplace. I haven't exchanged a birthday or Christmas gift with one of my brothers or sisters for as long as I can remember.

So again I dug down, and this one wasn't really too hard to figure out. In kindergarten at Loch Lomond elementary school, they used to do this thing called Secret Santa's Workshop, where children could go to a special room to shop for gifts for their family members. After making the selections, the orders were placed, and the gifts would arrive a week later and be delivered to each classroom. A day was set aside for the students to wrap each of their specially chosen gifts. To me it was fun, but looking back it was educational too: we learned how to think of others, and wrap gifts too.

I was ecstatic about this. In my mind there had never been a better idea. It was one of the few years that my sister Beta lived with us. Truth be told, Beta was born of a previous relationship in my mother's life, and was old enough to not like her mother starting a new family. I didn't know any better, I just thought it was how a sister was, but she was angry a lot. I guess my love for her was close to unconditional because I never thought a bad thing about her, but years later she confessed to being very nasty and angry about me and my father.

I couldn't wait to get my sister a gift. I had picked out a ring with a red stone. It was some little costume jewelry ring, but I thought it was special. I remember telling my mom and dad about it, and them telling me how thoughtful it was that I'd picked something out for my sister. I got my dad a little socket kit since he was a mechanic. It was a toy by his standards I'm sure, but it was made of metal and functional, and it showed that I knew what he did and who he was. I honestly can't remember what I got my mother, which is strange because she was my world back then.

So Christmas day came, and all I could think about was my sister's gift. I was so excited for her to open that package. When Beta finally opened her present from me, she was disgusted. She didn't hide it. She flat-out said, "What is this? I don't want this, and I would never wear it."

I broke into tears and jumped on my mom's lap. I was totally devastated. I didn't understand why she was so mad. How could I have been so off base? Even though I was hurt, she never apologized. I'm not saying it ruined my Christmas. I was six years old at the most. I'm sure I got over it quickly and played with my toys. However, I am sure now that it is why I'm petrified to give gifts.

I have to wonder how Beta escaped our

mother's beating technique to teach her the appreciation lesson my mom so gratefully gave me.

Years later, during my marriage, I'd obsess for months before any holiday, anniversary, or special occasion. I'd literally be sick about it, and still the ideas would never hit me until the day before. I was the ultimate Christmas Eve shopper. But to my merit, I'm not a gag gift giver or a practical gift giver. I put my heart and soul into it just like everything else I do. You're never going to get a meaningless article of clothing or a tool you already have four of from me. That is unless you make it perfectly clear that you want that and only that.

One year the ex insisted on a Dirt Devil-vacuum-type thing. Everyone advised me against it, but she'd insisted it was what she wanted. When presented with it she seemed happier than she had ever been, so I guess I did the right thing, but it felt so odd to me that I'll never forget it.

Then again, this chapter isn't about picking the gifts. It's about the reaction I have when giving and receiving them. That's why I'm a big fan of having things delivered when I'm not around.

In the last few months, I found myself in a gift exchange that I was sure I nailed. I was confident that I'd gotten it right. I was certain this person would love and be appreciative of the thought I'd put into my ideas, even if the ideas themselves weren't right.

Right up to the minute before I presented her with the gifts, I was fine. I thought, *Ha, I've beat this,* but then suddenly I couldn't look at her. I paced the room with tremendous nervousness as I waited for her to open them.

She was more than thankful, and it seemed like I had made the right choices. But even though I'd made it over that hurdle, I had another demon to face: I now had to receive the gifts from her.

She's much like me and takes this stuff seriously. I knew whatever she'd done, it would be flawless. Yet I stood there with the same fear.

The gifts were perfect.

While I know I showed some excitement and thankfulness, it wasn't half of what I felt inside.

I bet most people reading this think, *Wow, up until now I was with this guy to a certain extent, but freaking out about getting and giving gifts, that's crazier than the alien stuff in chapter eight.*

The interesting part is that, as I mentioned earlier, this is the first issue I've written about that I hadn't already tackled. The good thing is that, just in the time it took me to write this story, I feel like the problem may be gone or at least tamed. I'm actually excited about the idea of both getting a gift and presenting one to someone to see how it goes now that I have confronted myself with all of this.

When I started writing this book, I held on to the same theory I embrace when I write music. If I can make one person happy or feel better with each or any song I write, then I've accomplished my ultimate goal. I never thought that the one person who might feel better might be myself. Not that I'm proud of myself—I'm not big on pride—but I'm a little amused. I wonder if it counts if it's actually *me* that I affect.

Chapter Eleven
I won't ask you to do anything I wouldn't do

For most of my life I've been much more of a leader than a follower. A self-proclaimed leader in some cases, but a leader nonetheless.

Not that I have aspirations of world dominance like Hitler or Hussein, but I'd certainly love to have a hand in helping lead the world into a new way of thinking and usher in a new era of self-awareness like Bob Marley was on his way to doing.

But for now, I'm just a leader of a few rock-and-roll bands, and the owner of a candle company. Even though I may be seen as just the lead guitarist for rock-and-roll legend Bret Michaels's band, I've also earned the title of music director. That basically means that I'm in charge of that band also. Regardless of my experience as a leader, with every new opportunity comes the challenge of earning the trust of those I need to lead, so they will embrace being led. For the most part people are looking for "Something to Believe In" (yes, Bret, I just said that) or at least someone to believe in.

Obviously there are followers and there are leaders.

I prefer to lead, although I am a good learner. I take advice well, and I don't mind being given some direction, but if I have a choice, I'm more of a "toss me the keys and I'll get us there" kind of a guy.

No GPS required.

So, how do we become leaders? It's my opinion that natural-born leaders just have what it takes etched right into their DNA. But if you're not born with it, I believe it can be learned with hard work and a focused mind.

It doesn't always take book smarts or a formal education. While a degree never hurt anyone, I'm a big fan of street smarts and on-the-job training. I kind of like learning by being thrown to the wolves. That whole sink-or-swim concept just makes me dig in harder. Although this path usually brings anxiety and the feeling that you're having a heart attack, it's a lot more fun than sitting at a desk reading a manual. Consider it the businessman's version of riding exciting new roller coasters.

After twenty-seven years of being the leader of whatever band I've been in, I feel as if I've really got it down. The single most important thing I think that most aspiring head honchos miss is that, at all cost, you still have to be a team player.

You still have to get along with others.

It's clichéd, but even though I'm not an avid sports fan, I have to agree with the saying that a star quarterback is nothing without his team. Barking orders from a cushy office, never to be seen on the battlefield, gains nothing but resentment.

You also need to know your business inside and out. Not just the parts you dream about, but the boring stuff, the dirty stuff, the stuff no one seems to care about.

In my midtwenties, my then father-in-law asked me all kinds of questions about the music industry. He'd come to know me as the supposed expert when it came to the business of music, so why not? He was a huge music fan and was thirsty for knowledge. I often had to tell him I didn't have the answers he was looking for, and quite honestly, his questions seemed unimportant to the specific path I was on. I knew what I needed to get my job done.

At first this didn't bother me, but as I got older it became embarrassing. I certainly had blinders on. You can't have the respect or trust of others if you don't have broad knowledge of the field you're supposed to be an expert in. So I upped my game a little and tried to soak in a bit more than what I specifically wanted to know.

The music biz has basically written its own rules though and it's extremely hard to define right or wrong or for that matter, who holds the authority's and the true knowledge. To understand this I'm gonna try to explain first how the wrong person can be perceived as the leader, so try to focus this may not make sense at first, but there's a reason to my rhyme.

***

In the case of being in a band, at any level, there's usually the arrogant and / or lazy member who doesn't want to help with the physical labor like moving the gear or setting up the stage. Somehow that person ends up being perceived as, and then actually becoming, the so-called leader.

I've said it before: perception is everything.

I've seen situations where this happens because whoever isn't helping load gear ends up having free time to talk, so naturally if someone has a question, they ask the guy who's not doing anything. Presto! They become the instant spokesperson for the group. Suddenly someone else needs something, and the last guy who talked to our newfound leader simply points to the guy he just talked to and says, "That's the guy you need to talk to."

This can all happen in a matter of seconds at a high school talent show, dirty old bar, or backyard party. It happens on other levels too. It even happened to KISS—you can actually read all about this type of thing in Paul Stanley's book.

But don't read this as me saying that being lazy will make you a leader. That lazy guy might be perceived as the leader temporarily, but it won't last. This never works. This type of leader becomes resented really fast, and soon enough they come to band practice on Tuesday night to find their gear in the driveway and that they have been replaced.

This, however, is not a "what not to do," but rather a "what to do right" type of story.

In high school, I had worked at a local mom-and-pop music store called Music City. The owner, Steve, and his right-hand man, Kevin, were more fathers to me than my own. They spent time teaching me about gear, how to repair gear, and all things music. But they also spent hours just talking about life. In my very small world in 1988, they and that store were all I seemed to need.

When Steve opened a second store that his wife ran, they sent me to work there. For a while it was great, but eventually times got bad and she sold it. I was heartbroken. No longer was it a family business; now some guy I thought was an idiot owned it. I tried to hang in there for about a week, but I finally had to quit.

I'd only been out of school a year and still living at home. The problem was that I needed a job to keep up with my guitar-buying habit. Not only that, but Mom and Dad were very much of the you-must-have-a-job mentality.

In search of employment, I went into another independently owned store, Melodee Music, and introduced myself. I told them if they ever needed help, I had several years' experience in the field of mom-and-pop music stores. They were in Loudoun County, a richer, more upscale area compared to Manassas. I remember thinking they'd never call me back.

A few days later they did call and asked if I wanted the job. As excited as I was, I also felt an overwhelming sense of betrayal to the other music store. While they had sold the one store, the main one that Kevin and Steve ran was still there. Was I doing the right thing? This haunted me for a long time. The concepts of loyalty and do-what's-best-for-yourself are two of the most confusing things to try to blend. Both are incredibly important to your character and work ethic, but sometimes it's flat-out impossible to have them coexist.

Then came my first day at work. My new boss was a guy named Rob. I never gave him enough credit, but he may be the unsung hero of my entire life story.

He was the youngest son of the family that

owned the store, and wasn't a huge fan of the music industry. Don't get me wrong: Rob loved music, and I'm eternally grateful that he introduced me to artists like Lyle Lovett, but he wasn't an obsessed fanatic and didn't even play an instrument. To him it was just the family business.

But even though he wasn't invested in music, he was a great businessman. Rob showed me the ropes, and then he turned to me and said, "I'll never ask you to do something I haven't done myself."

Wow, that was big, powerful, and profound. Eleven words came at me in a split second with more meaning than an entire college education.

While many of the moments I've shared with you evolved me over time, this was different.

This was instant.

Everything changed right then and there.

My respect and lack of respect for all kinds of people shifted in that moment. It's the businessman's version of walk-a-mile-in-his-shoes at the simplest level.

From that point on, I addressed everything with this attitude, and it helped me gain respect from those I was trying to lead. Eventually, this concept evolved into what I consider the biggest piece of advice, wisdom, or knowledge I could pass on to anyone, in the music biz or any profession, if you're struggling to truly own your own destiny.

The music business is hard. Artists, bands, and talented individuals sit around and waste their talent waiting on someone to invest in them—waiting on an agent, a manager, or that big record deal.

As I grew older, I thought about what Rob had said to me. I applied that attitude to finance. Meaning, why would I ask anyone else to invest in my music career if I wasn't willing to do so myself? I took all the money I had and invested in my band's shows, be it drum risers or backdrops or homemade pyro. I even eventually funded my own record, videos, and radio campaigns.

Through all the years, it paid off.

People saw my dedication, my work ethic, and my desire. For many years, I'd drive the gear, unload it, set it up myself, and then do the gig.

I went from wide-eyed child with a dream to being part of one of the most respected—not to mention highest-paid—bands in my region. It wasn't easy. It took years. But it did happen.

Through the years, I also opened a recording studio and rehearsal hall, started a record label, and most recently started Shining Sol Candle Company.

Each of these ventures just couldn't have happened without those words Rob Mock spoke to me.

Here comes the fun part.

Fast-forward about fifteen years.

I'm playing guitar with a rock-and-roll legend and one of my childhood heroes, Bret Michaels. We are doing one of our first shows together, on Memorial Day weekend in Nashville, Tennessee, for a sold-out crowd of well over 25,000 people. I walk to the loading dock, and Bret, *who does not have to lift a finger again in his life other than to buckle the seat belt in his private plane*, is attaching decorations to our speaker cabinets.

I walk over and say, "Bret, why don't you let me do that?"

He was very kind and declined, responding that he liked doing it.

As we got closer over the years, I would and still do inquire about his amazing success and how he beat all the odds to not only become the icon of a generation but an incredible businessman both in and outside of the music business. One day I brought up the situation on the loading dock.

I asked, "Why didn't you have one of us do it?"

Wait for it . . .

He said, "Never ask someone to do something you won't or haven't done yourself."

And history repeated itself. Like God's way of making sure I remembered that lesson.

Although that last line was a perfect tag to the end this story with, I have to take it one step further.

This lesson has been instrumental to me as a parent as well. My two boys are the single most important team I will ever have the honor to lead. Right down to something as simple as getting them to try new foods or clean their room, I take that role to heart and keep that motto in mind. It doesn't work if you won't do or haven't tried the things you're pushing your kids to do, and it helps if they see you do it.

Children are like sponges, soaking up everything—the good *and* the bad right from day one. Mine have challenged me every step of the way, and being able to lead by example and honestly say, "Yes, I have done this," sometimes has been the only way to get them to follow.

I challenge you to be thoughtful of the moments and places where your life changed on a dime.

Who knew that nineteen-year-old me would get a life lesson in parenting, business, and finance the first day on the job at a little family-owned music store in Sterling, Virginia?

Chapter Twelve
In Comedy lies Depth

While many people hold athletes, authors, rock stars, and entrepreneurs up as heroes, it's rather unusual to hear someone call out a comedian as heroic.

Sure, there are exceptions. Those who break out of the stand-up circuit and go on to become legendary actors like the amazing Robin Williams, who tragically passed away prior to me finishing this book, are considered influential and obtain hero   status.

Comedians are some of the most deep, interesting, and thought-provoking beings I have ever met. Interestingly enough, although they bring us great joy, I often see pain in their eyes.

Comedians study the world around them so deeply, looking for whatever it takes to make you smile, that they find the darkest of the dark, and it hurts their heart terribly. It eventually eats at their soul.

They look in places we don't, and find things we won't.

Much like newscasters, they need to be very aware of what is going on right here and now in the world. Oftentimes it's tragedy that warrants a humorous moment to help us cope with it—to challenge us to see it from a different angle.

It takes a skilled person to cheer us up on our darkest days. In the world we live in, it can seem near impossible. I commend them for finding a way, and if they touch even one of us with that profound skill, then they've passed on a gift. Dave Chappelle is a true genius who touched on some very controversial stuff that could make you feel uncomfortable if you were watching it with people you didn't know. He dug so deep into his art, and when he felt it was taken the wrong way, it sent him spiraling out of the biz. Much like musicians or poets with their lyrics and verses, comedians lay it all on the line. They share feelings and vulnerabilities with the public, only disguised as jokes. That can play some brutal tricks on your mind, I assume. One time I had written a song called "Face to Face." One of the lyrics was:

I'm sorry about this baggage
That comes along with me

But I never did think
You'd get so close
That you would have to see

I played it for a fellow musician by the name of Ned, and his reply was, "Wow, you really put yourself out there."

That moment is when I realized artists are a fragile and different breed. I didn't think I was doing anything different than anyone else would, but in fact, I was doing what most people can't comprehend. I was being honest. Exposing my wounds and weaknesses, only I did it in lyric form.

Another deceased comedian I loved was Mitch Hedberg. My friend Chuck and I discovered him one day while scrolling through the satellite radio channels. He became the sole reason for our existence for some time. He too was a tortured soul who saw the world completely differently. Anytime we can push outside our comfort zone to explore something in a different way, we win as far as I'm concerned. Comedians help us do that. Mitch excelled at it. On the rare evening that I have free time, I'll pick a comedy club over live music or any other kind of event. Try it, if you haven't. Maybe you'll walk away with a new view on something. I always do.

My friends and peers have always commended me for being fearless. From my earliest days, I'd be the first to jump in the creek or off a roof, or climb a tree. I was that kid your mom lectured you about.

If Pete jumped off a bridge, would you?

Life has always been so interesting, I didn't want to miss a thing. That translated into my ability to chase my dreams. I was never afraid of failure in my pursuit of a career in music. I never even considered a fallback plan. When I was twenty, the grunge era hit the music scene, and for a very short time in history, the feel-good rock and roll that I loved took a backseat to the dark and gloomy Seattle sound. Only a few bands, like Bon Jovi, Van Halen, and Poison, continued to tour the big arenas throughout that era. I didn't know what to do, because I couldn't fake it. I wasn't going to wear combat boots and flannel, and complain about my life. Although I did have a pair of silver Doc Martens that I loved.

So, Chuck and my friend Paul (aka Bear) and I opened up a professional recording studio and rehearsal facility in hopes of staying in the music biz. It was the type of thing you find in LA, Nashville, and New York, not in a small town in Virginia. And it certainly wasn't the kind of task that twenty-year-old kids took on. But I talked the guys into it, and blindly we jumped headfirst into being business owners. People thought I was crazy, but it worked. The studio was called Clear Sound Music Center. We really created a scene, and before we knew it, everyone was hanging out there. We were all making records and living the dream in our own local musical hot spot.

Technically, we only stayed open for four years. My mother passed away. I was about to get married, the dark cloud of grunge had passed, and my band Some Odd Reason had landed a record deal. I was going to get to live my real dream and tour the country as a professional musician. I had to let the studio go. Clear Sound Music Center is a part of my life I will never forget. It was before the age of cell phones with cameras, and I wasn't one to keep a regular camera around. I regret not taking many photographs of that amazing time, but we were too busy making music to think about anything else.

I've taken lots of huge leaps of faith. I'm not afraid to open doors when I don't know what's on the other side. It's who I am. You can't fake that.

But even living the dream comes with challenges. Some Odd Reason went through member changes, and the music scene changed again. Our style of music had been replaced by nu metal, which included groups like Limp Bizkit, Godsmack, and Slipknot. While I was and am a fan of that music, it's not what I bring to the party.

So I started looking for new doors again.

We morphed the band into a party cover band and went back to playing three sets of music a night in small bars. Since music was all I knew, I had to make it work as a career, not a hobby. But as with everything in my life back then, I wanted something more than I was living. Not necessarily more glamorous. I didn't need to be rich. I just wanted to taste life on a grander scale. I had seen glimpses of the larger world while on tour with Some Odd Reason, so I knew what was out there. I wanted desperately for my world to be bigger. I wanted to find the door to the next level, not just in music, but in life.

In the '70s and early '80s, bands could play house gigs and do the same venue three or four nights a week and make a living. Probably the most famous story of this is of my friend Dee Snider and his band Twisted Sister. During that time, they raked it in as a cover band in the bars on Long Island. (Note that by "raked it in," I mean they made enough money to not have day jobs; any one of them will tell you they weren't buying mansions and planes.) But again this option had all but disappeared by the time I was out playing professionally. Most venues stopped having bands Monday through Thursday nights, and even on weekends there would be multiple bands on the bill and money was split between three bands per night.

Everyone I knew thought I was crazy. But I found a way to play six nights a week in any and every bar that would have me. At that point in my career, I was just a guitar player and songwriter. My vocals were so bad that I wasn't even allowed to have a mic on stage.

Seriously.

I wrote a song called "Big Rock Guitars" that sums up where I was at that time in my life. The lyrics went:

I've paid my dues
On these lonely roads in the middle of the night.
I know every single exit sign on I-95.
I've lived my life in and out
Of these dingy local bars,
From the bottom of the Florida Keys
To the middle of Baltimore.
I didn't do it for the wine, the women,
The money, or fancy cars.
From the moment that I heard that sound,
I fell in love
With those big rock guitars

I must have made this same old ride
A million times or more.
Been laughed at, lied to,
Yelled at, cried to,
Burnt to the core.
I've seen some things
I must confess, but I don't think I should.

Ain't never lived the glamorous life
But it's made for Hollywood.

I was approaching thirty and married at the time. Most people had long since quit the music business if they hadn't truly made it yet. To me, as long as I was getting the bills paid, I had made it. But something else was happening too.

The one guy who believed in me, my lawyer Ron Beinstock, told me that I should learn to sing—be the front man. I needed to find a way to be in control of what was happening in our live shows—to sell the audience my story straight from the horse's mouth.

Switching guitar players or drummers in a band is one thing; switching the voice and the guy who does all the talking—well, that changes everything.

The thought of this was comedic to my fellow musicians. I couldn't sing. My friends laughed in my face; they didn't even try to hide it. Most were at least honest, even if it was brutal, and said, "You cannot do this." My family was scared to death.

I was well aware that I couldn't sing. But there was a whole world of opportunities if I could just admit it, suck it up, and walk through that door ready and willing to learn. My lawyer gave me the number of the biggest of bigwig Broadway vocal coaches. This coach had helped Jon Bon Jovi and the

Rolling Stones, to name a few. Serious talent. For nine months I went to New York City, sometimes driving 250 miles from home to take a half-hour lesson, then driving 250 miles back home that same day. I remember how scared I was making that first drive. It wasn't the drive that scared me—I could do that in my sleep—it was what would happen at this lesson. For the first time, I was afraid.

The voice coach, Don Lawrence, had an impressive résumé and platinum records all over the walls of his Manhattan office. This was the big leagues, and I couldn't sing a lick. I stood at his door with more fear than I had ever had in my life. I'd never failed at anything, and most of my peers had been very clear that this would be my fall from grace, and they were all going to be sitting in front-row seats to watch.

Pushing my fear aside, I walked in and put everything on the line. Within ten minutes under Lawrence's guidance, I learned more than I'd ever dreamed I would. I was so incredibly positive that I would become a singer that I sang every KISS, Van Halen, Bon Jovi, and Poison song I knew at the top of my lungs on my four-hour drive home that day, and haven't stopped since. My childhood friend, John, rode with me to New York City that day. I've never apologized for singing so loud during those four hours back to Virginia. I'm surprised he ever spoke to me again.

While just walking through that door was scary, I was an adult and needed to support my family. I couldn't just be a student. I had to perform to pay the bills. It takes a long time to learn how to sing, and a longer time to learn how to become a front man. Most people rehearse in their basements for years. Then they spend time with their high school or weekend garage band working their way up to it. I didn't have that luxury. I literally had to book gigs and go for it. That, my friends, is scary!

I learned to sing night after night in every bar in Virginia that would book me. I had to practice right there in my hometown, in front of all those who were waiting for my failure. Honestly, at first it looked like it was going to go that way. It was rough. Many nights I knew I was doing awful and wanted to run off the stage, but it forced me to become a better front man.

I wasn't good. And unlike the positive feedback I was used to getting for my guitar playing, there was no chance that anyone was going to come at the end of the night to tell me how well I sang. In survival mode, I learned to entertain real fast. Thank God, I was heavily influenced by KISS over the years.

Eventually I got it down, and did what at the time I considered a miracle. I'd reinvented myself in front of a live audience, and then toured as a cover band. If reality TV had been a part of pop culture at that time, I could have been its biggest star.

I had to bury the name Some Odd Reason and took a lesson from two of my favorite acts, Bon Jovi and Van Halen. And the band EVICK was born. Off I went with my new life and career as a singer. It was unheard of, but I was all over the country, from Virginia to Los Angeles, and New York City to the Florida Keys, singing in my rock-and-roll band.

I had looked uncertainty right in the face, opened the door to the unknown, and walked right through it. Sometimes you have to dig down and have the faith to take that chance.

So how does all of this tie into comedians? Where is the magic moment in all of this? It has to do with comedian Jim Carrey, who is iconic, legendary even. He'd made a name for himself doing over-the-top and borderline obnoxious roles in movies like *Ace Ventura*. Then he took on a role in a movie called *The Truman Show*. This was way before reality TV was the gigantic success it is today. It was in 1998, and basically the movie almost prophesied the world we now live in.

For those not familiar, *The Truman Show* is about a child who from day one was filmed in a make-believe world in a giant movie studio. He was completely unaware of the situation. Who he thought were his parents were just actors. The town was a giant prop. His friends weren't his friends, but rather hired for the parts. Even the sun and moon were images on a screen set far enough away that he just didn't know any different. The movie is pure brilliance, and while hysterical, it really had dark undertones of religious, and political, misguidance. To me, the message was huge. But as with any media, we all take away our own impressions. *Star Wars*, for example, to me is not a science fiction movie at all. It's the greatest tale of political and religious turmoil wrapped up in a giant love story. It just so happens that the setting is in outer space.

In *The Truman Show*, as Truman got older he could feel his world getting smaller, and just like anyone of any faith who follows the rules of that faith without question, eventually he sees the cracks in what he's been taught and begins to at the very least become curious. Eventually, he finds his way to the wall at the end of the movie studio, and is met by a set of steps leading to the door that's been hiding the rest of the world from him.

I remember the anticipation. I can still feel it now. That scene is truly amazing yet so simple, and even though I knew the outcome and the moral of the story, to have it visualized was so powerful. There is a moment when he's talking to the creator of the show, who tries to play God by use of a mic and loud PA system to seem as though his voice is coming from the heavens. The creator says, "You belong here with me." He's trying to selfishly get

Truman to stay, so his life can go on as the producer of the hit television show. He then tells Truman, "You're a star!" The producer was trying to convince Truman that what he had was enough, that there is no reason to leave the safety of his little town. No matter what you do, do not walk through that door.

It's not so different from people telling their entertainer friends that being a local star is enough, to accept that and not risk it by chasing the bigger dream. Or advising someone to stay in college or pursue a job they are unhappy in, just for the security   of   it. It sounds terrible, but it reminds me that weaker-minded people will always try to keep you down.

I've faced it my whole life.

The "You're never going to make it" comments.

And "People from here don't get out of here."

They don't fear for your failure; they just don't have the drive to succeed themselves. So they try to convince you, out of their own selfishness, to be afraid. To not walk through that door.

In the last moment of *The Truman Show*, Jim Carrey as Truman smiles and says, "In case I don't see you, good afternoon, good evening, and good night." Then he walks through that door.

Think about it: the idea was that through that door was the complete unknown. Imagine being alive and awake and seeing the gates to heaven, or hell. Imagine a portal, a Stargate. There it was for him to walk through.

Would you?

I certainly would.

It was incredibly inspiring for a musician from a small town. I remember begging him in my mind to walk through that door. When he did, I felt so relieved and so excited. I said to myself, "YES! Always walk through any door. Pete, for the rest of your life, always walk through the door."

And I have. Over and over again.

I did it with the studio.

I did it when I shut the studio down to sign the record deal.

I did it choosing to sing.

Even joining rock legend Bret Michaels's band was a complete unknown. I had never done anything where I wasn't the boss and complete leader. It was foreign territory for me. A risk. A chance.

And, of course, becoming a parent was the biggest unknown door I've ever walked through. It has led to a hundred other doors I've had to open. An amazing and frightening experience.

Most recently, I did it again when I started my newest venture, Shining Sol Candle Company. A year before we were open for business, I knew nothing about the candle industry. But I had an interest and I was inspired to succeed.

Just like Truman, I walked right through that door.

Writing this book is walking through another door. I have no idea how to do this. I'm a musician. A songwriter. A storyteller. I've been told by too many people over the years that I should write a book, so I'm turning that handle and opening that door right this second.

In actuality, this book is probably my scariest door opening of all time, because I've spilled my heart out on these pages completely unfiltered for any and every one to read, leaving the story for my children's kids and the entire universe to know. Could you or would you walk through that door?

It's rare that I rely on anyone to help me through anything, but writer Nancy Naigle has been more than a friend—she is the reason this book will ever get done. Just like Jim Carrey's character in *The Truman Show*, she has walked and continues to walk through doors. While we were instant friends from day one, over the years, she's shared her amazing journey with me. Just in the time I've known her, she was a successful but part-time writer, she chose to walk through the door, leaving the security of a career in banking to become a full-time writer, and has had several chart topping books.

Obviously Bret Michaels is a door opener as well: he does it all day, every day. He's totally fearless when diving into the unknown. I'm grateful to have real relationships with people whose lives are like the inspirational stories usually saved for Hollywood.

My life and the reason for writing this book is one of soul searching—almost a hunt for spirituality. Over the last several years as one of my best friends, and recently on a much higher level, an amazing woman has walked this path with me. Her drive to be a better person and her understanding of what really matters should earn her sainthood one day. She already has her angel wings, even though they are just tattooed on her back. And recently she has walked through some doors that have been waiting to be opened by her for a long time. Her courage, when she believed for the longest time that she had none, has been an amazing gift to watch develop and I believe she would say, like me, the personal reward for walking through those doors is indescribable.

While this book is not about her, Bret, or Nancy, much like Nancy and Bret, she has opened doors her whole life, ones that most people would never even consider. These are just a few examples of other people in my life who inspire me to open my doors. I encourage you to find the people around you who practice such things. Let them be your inspiration to do the same.

As I was writing these final chapters, the

tattooed angel stumbled upon a video of Jim Carrey giving a commencement speech at the 2014 Maharishi University of Management graduation and insisted that I watch.

If you haven't heard of it, it's a university that uses a new approach called consciousness-based education, where meditation plays a key role in the studies. Mr. Carrey gives a chilling inspirational speech. He is incredibly open about the pain comedians go through. He is very honest about his own ego and his need to feed it. And he is brilliantly inspiring from his first words. Almost twenty years after he filmed *The Truman Show*, I found myself totally inspired by him again, and his main message in this speech, if you had to sum it up in under five words, is "Walk through the door."

Here's your chance to stretch your reality. To believe in yourself and challenge yourself.

What door is in front of you?

Will you walk through it?

Chapter Thirteen
Your Mom Did That?

It's funny to me that here I am, basically at the end of this book, and my friend Nancy (who, as I mentioned in the last chapter, has been a huge inspiration and help in getting this book done) was kind of pushing for a little more content. But I had been writing for years and really felt like I'd reached the end. Then I looked up and realized this is chapter thirteen.

What?

I'm not ending my first book with thirteen chapters. Call me superstitious—perhaps I am—so now my last chapter, which I've been excited to write since I penned chapter one, will now be chapter fourteen and this wonderfully strange story will forever be chapter thirteen. So, between superstition and Nancy encouraging me to tell a few more tales, I was suddenly struck by an unbelievable story that now I cannot understand why I was going leave out in the first place. Indeed, it was a moment that changed my life. It also has had a big impact on how I parent my children.

I've actually told this story many times, but for some reason, it never made sense until now to put it in the book and share it with you.

My mother was a unique woman, to say the least. Plagued with health issues from the time I was born and probably long before, she was at times as mean, violent, and hateful as anyone I've ever met. Keep in mind that I work in the music business, and I truly believe I've seen the worst of the worst when it comes to hatefulness and damaged human character in general.

I have early memories of coming home from school to things like my mother tossing her record player lid at my sister's head in a fit of anger. On that day in particular, someone called the cops. When the police showed up, my mom charged out of the house with her hands in front of her, yelling at the police officer to cuff her and take her to jail because she didn't give a shit. I was ushered away to the neighbors, as I explained in chapter nine, so I don't know how much further she pushed it.

I remember standing there watching and thinking, *Wow, my mom just stood up to the cops. She's not afraid of anything.*

That may have been an equally defining moment for me, paving a path for my own rebellion against the system, and my direct lack of concern for authority. If a frail, sick old woman could defy the police, I certainly didn't have to fear them either.

She may not have been gentle, but what my mom was, was loyal to a fault. My mom was either your best friend or your worst enemy—simply no in between. She was also a realist. She just didn't BS anyone about anything. Again, honorable, but that meant even her kids got the truth. Always.

I might add that my mother was also one whose mind and opinion were unchangeable. Once she made a decision, even if she was proven wrong, she'd stick with that decision until her last breath. If she said the sky was green, it was without a doubt green.

When I was five years old and about to head into kindergarten, I was with my mother at the Grand Union grocery store. It was a Thursday morning in August.

A quick digression: Back in those days, there was a consistency to life that doesn't seem to exist anymore.

Grand Union on Thursdays.

Happy Days on ABC on Tuesday nights.

Dinner at 5:30 p.m. every day.

Sometimes I long for that routine again. These days, I haven't woken up in the same bed three days in a row for ten years. Dinner is when I have time to eat, and any TV show I want to watch is purchased on iTunes and watched in the middle of the night when I'm suffering from insomnia and have finally given up on the thought that I might sleep that night.

Getting back to the story, I was excited about kindergarten. I had no idea what to expect or that for the first time I was going to have the power to influence and also be influenced by my peers. It's funny to think peer pressure and the need to be dominant starts at such an early age, but it does. From the second we play with our neighborhood friends, we are officially under the influence of our peers.

My mother actually worked at the Grand Union, but on this day we were just customers. As we stood in the checkout line, some of her friends were there; everyone's chatting, and all seems normal and happy. Suddenly, out of nowhere, she turns to me in front of everyone and says, "Pete, I'm gonna tell you something and you need to keep this to yourself. Do not tell your friends or anyone when you start school, not even your teachers."

I remember thinking it must be something very important. And I've never forgotten what she said.

Word for word.

"Pete, Santa Claus, the Easter bunny, the tooth fairy—it's all fake. None of it is real. You'll still get your gifts. We will still decorate eggs and celebrate these things but . . . none of it's real."

What is a five-year-old boy supposed to do with that information?

A part of my innocence was clearly lost right then and there in a checkout line of a grocery store in Manassas, Virginia.

I am notorious for not looking excited, no matter if the situation is good or bad. I have somewhat of a poker face.

Interestingly enough, I seem to be more known for my smile and animated faces onstage than my talent as a musician, but offstage you could hand me a billion dollars and I'd look the same as the moment I found out my mom or dad passed away. My point? I must have been making that poker face my whole life because I still remember all the people around me and my mother seemed more shocked that I looked like I didn't care than at the fact that a mother had just dumped that information on her child.

The truth is, I really think I *didn't* care. I don't remember being shocked. It was almost like I knew. I wonder if all of us know, if we are born with truth, and our humanity feeds us the lie, then universally as a species we live the lie.

I remember having the "Is Santa real?" conversation with my friends Mike and John a few years later.. Mike believed; John did not. I think

John came to the conclusion on his own. His older brother and sister might have helped guide his thoughts, although I remember a bit of uncertainty in him when it came to this topic, like maybe he didn't have all the facts, but his gut told him Santa was fake. Mike explained in minute detail why he believed, complete with stories of hearing a man's voice give a "Ho, ho, ho" in his own home on Christmas Eve while he was supposed to be sleeping. I could have spilled Mom's message to the both of them. I thought better of it. I knew that letting them both believe what they wanted to believe, even with a degree of uncertainty, made them both happier than laying down my cards. Plus maybe part of me was uncertain after hearing Mike's airtight defense of Santa's existence. Maybe he was right.

Sometimes it's okay to let someone else be right. This is a theory I have always subscribed to even at an early age. Our own fairy tales give us a sense of security. In many ways, is that not what religion really is? Christianity, much like Santa Claus, gives us something to believe in and also a reason to fear. Santa and Jesus both give us the illusion of safety by letting us know something bigger and stronger than us is watching over us. Just as kids fear Santa may not bring toys, adults believe Jesus will send you to hell. Jesus appears to be the adult version of Santa Claus; seems like simple math to me.

Interestingly enough, the sentiment of letting Mike believe his version of Santa without me trying to ruin his day has carried on with me into my adulthood in a very powerful way. I honestly think that letting people believe things that make them happy truly doesn't hurt anyone. I had a girlfriend once who was incredibly smart. Her dad was a true genius, a scientist and inventor. These traits ran in her blood. I will go to my grave saying she was brilliant; however, she loved to correct people. She was almost passionate about it. I remember one time fighting very aggressively with her about the topic.

She had felt the need to correct someone while we stood in a large group of friends.

"Just let them be right," I'd say.

"Why?"

"Because they are happy believing, and it doesn't affect you in any way. Why crush that little bit of happiness in someone you don't even know that well?"

I don't know if she ever understood, and maybe her mission is to set people straight here on earth, who knows?

While I am neither naive or all-knowing, due to my lifelong paranoia and skepticism, it seems to me that being blind or naive is easier than being cursed with having all the answers. The phrase "ignorance is bliss" is part of the psychology used by whoever created the kind of religions that are made to make people feel safe and protected. While I disagree with the concept, I do understand it. However, whoever invented Catholicism, baptism, and the "Jesus will get you" religions, well, I still have no idea of their reasoning. But due to our fear instincts, these sadistic, power-hungry control freaks sure pulled one over on our species and are still doing it.

It may seem like I went off topic a little, but you should be able to see where I'm going pretty easily: my predetermined lack of faith that a fat man in red would be bringing me toys may have directly affected my life long struggle to believe a shirtless, long-haired guy would show me the road to heaven.

Now, with that being said, a child does need heroes, and since my overly honest mom took the normal ones away from me, my five-year-old self was left with no other option than believing in KISS. They were tangible. I could prove they were real, and to a five-year-old whose nonreligious parents weren't buying into the hype that these four face-painted rock and rollers were devil worshipers, I'd struck gold. I had all the heroes I needed at my disposal in my room with my posters and record player.

I also believe that the Santa thing is one of the reason I held on so tightly to *Star Wars* and still do to this day. It was full of magic and myth and all the things that had been taken away from me that day in Grand Union. Instead of a sleigh I had the Millennium Falcon, instead of Rudolph I had Chewbacca, and instead of Jesus I had Obi-Wan Kenobi. A fair trade in my book.

I have also always considered the Fourth of July to be my favorite of the holidays. I believe that this is because it's not tied to any myth or religion and isn't associated with gift giving. It's a pure and obvious observation and celebration of our country and our freedom, which always seemed powerful to me. But I have to wonder if my initial interest in the Fourth of July was because it wasn't one of the holidays on my mother's list of fakes.

I believe my mom's news that day helped me for most of my life. I never had to feel the letdown of the truth after putting all my faith in it, and I think it helped me to not be afraid of other things, like the boogeyman.

If there's no Santa, there's no boogeyman, right?

While it's no secret that I believe there are extraterrestrials and the possibility of the supernatural, I've also been skeptical my whole life. I've wanted to believe in everything, but also need it to be proven and indisputable. I'd like to think of myself as the world's most skeptical believer. Now consider this: what must I know about the extraterrestrial phenomenon to say with certainty I believe? That's another book all its own.

***

Over the years I have certainly enjoyed the look on people's faces when I tell them what my mom did. To be honest, it never gets old.

However, once my kids were born, this became a much bigger issue, a struggle that tugged at me from before they were old enough to even know who Santa was. All my emotions were turned around when I was considering how to let this play out with my children. The mother of my children and several others I discussed this with seemed to have a universal go-to line when dealing with this issue: when kids start to question such things, you basically tell them, "If you believe, then it's real." At first, I was furious—that seemed like such a cop-out. I thought I would absolutely stick to my guns and pass my mother's message on to my kids. Then I began to watch the innocence of my own children, and wow, everything changed. I now tend to live life by the motto "If I believe, then it's real."I began to ask people how it affected them when they found out about such myths and legends not being real as they got older.

To my surprise, no one seemed to have had a traumatic experience discovering the truth. Then I started thinking of how different I'd been made to feel my whole life, and of all things, I didn't want to pass that on to Gavin and Jacob. So while my entire life I'd planned on telling my kids, as my mom had told me, that there was no Santa, among other things, I suddenly just couldn't. But was this hypocrisy? Was I now my very own fear-driven church? The thought of holding Santa over my sons' heads in hopes of them behaving was suddenly a pretty good idea. Catholicism and the mighty southern Baptists made a little more sense to me.

This may all sound silly, but I stressed about it, and I think I did so internally, because if you ask my ex or family, they probably don't recall any of it ever happening. I'd learned to internalize my battles about raising my children because my opinion was never the popular vote. I considered letting the kids believe in Santa, but telling them not to be afraid, that bad or good, he will come. Then I realized that would cause more problems than good; why would Santa's rules be different in our home? It was clearly all or nothing in this situation. Looking back, I feel like I did the right thing: the idea of Santa brought so much joy to Gavin and Jacob. Selfishly, I embraced the innocence of it so much I can't even put it into words. But it was an interesting struggle feeling like I started my own hypocritical religion in my own house. An interesting lesson on building a society. When you start a family, that's basically what you do, right? You start your own society, or community.

As I write this, my oldest son, Gavin, is twelve, and yesterday was Halloween. Jacob still eagerly anticipated and happily participated in the festivities.

Gavin opted out.

I spent the day on a tour bus in Memphis, Tennessee, somewhat heartbroken that Gavin had seemingly grown up in the blink of an eye. If Halloween is over for him, that has to mean Santa is too.

I know he started to show cracks in his belief last year as he began to ask questions that were hard to answer, like how Santa gets in our house without a chimney, and does he not get sick from eating cookies in every single house?

Suddenly, my heart stopped as I thought of Jacob in his Halloween costume, and Gavin not. How do we keep Jacob believing, when his older brother, who has a passion for ruining his younger brother's day, will soon be armed (if he's not already) with the truth about Santa?

How have families done this for centuries? I began to think I should have gone with my original plan and told the truth from the beginning, and protected Jacob from an early letdown. Maybe I still have enough influence on Gavin to have him co-

conspire in the big lie with me and his mother. Unfortunately, this is happening in real time as I write this, so I don't know what I'm going to do. So yeah. Welcome to my life.

Thank you, Mom, for being honest, and throwing the biggest wrench in parenting anyone could ever throw.

Pete, there is no Santa. Are you kidding me?

Still shaking my head.

***

Interestingly enough, Gavin made mention of things over the last year that also made me realize, eventually technology will kill Santa, along with the Easter bunny and the tooth fairy, forever. Gavin had a plan last year to simply capture video from his iPad of our living room on Christmas Eve to catch Santa, if he really existed.

My thoughts first went to the excitement I had in my kid's detective skills. But then I thought, wow, all it takes is one kid not giving his parents a heads-up and doing something like this all on his own, taking a video of his parents putting the presents under the tree and loading it on YouTube, and everything changes, and I mean *everything*. I'm surprised it hasn't happened yet, or maybe it has and I'm just too self-absorbed to realize it.

When I was a kid, we didn't have those tools at

our disposal, and if the family happened to have a video camera, your parents would easily catch on to what you were doing and make you turn it off. These days, kids have all kinds of devices that are exclusively their own. As a musician, it takes me back to the moment MTV debuted and the "Video Killed the Radio Star" video and ushered in a new level of musical consciousness; our one-dimensional music all of a sudden had two dimensions. On a larger scale, it reminds me of the conspiracy theorists who constantly remind us that our society would collapse if the world's governments told us the truth about extraterrestrial life. How, in an instant, all the world's currency and religion would be rendered useless in the blink of an eye.

It sure is a lot to think about for a chapter that started with a five-year-old boy in a grocery store, don't you think? But again, this whole book is supposed to inspire your mind to explore everything you can possibly dream up.

On a side note, it's very important that I point out that just because I seem to be bashing Christianity, I'm not, I openly have issues with many of today's organized religions, but I have been on a spiritual search my whole life, due to my life experiences I've found it hard to have blind faith in anything but I'm closer now than I've ever been to having such faith, but it's a work in progress, through the years though I've had two people, Sean and Kyle guide me, inspire me and answer many questions that keep me up at night. I just wanted to take a minute in this book to acknowledge them and there help, and again explain that bashing any organized religion does not mean I'm bashing God.

Chapter Fourteen
Sometimes a Rainbow Is Better Than a Pot of Gold

It's been more than five years since I started writing this book. But even on that first day I sat down to write, I knew this story was how I wanted to wrap up my book.

Much like the *Star Wars* prequels where we knew it ended with Anakin Skywalker becoming Darth Vader, I didn't know what the whole story would look like, but I knew this would be my grand finale. This recollection is full of coincidence and irony—or fate—depending on what you believe.

Although this one takes place a little bit later in my life than many of the other stories, its impact and the outcome are still amazing to me. It definitely contains the moments that made me who I am today. Besides, many of you are reading this because you know me as a rock-and-roll musician, so I had to put some rock and roll in the book eventually. This is for you.

I was thirteen in the summer of 1986. Moving from middle school to high school, my life was consumed with nothing but rock-and-roll dreams. My days were spent primarily on two things: playing guitar and riding my bike.

I was big into BMX bikes and had I truly known that people would eventually make careers out of riding them, I might have gone down a different path. I seriously loved them as much as rock and roll, and I was pretty good at some of the crazy freestyle tricks. My friends and I found dirt trails behind a shopping center that we couldn't get enough of and spent hours building quarter pipes on street corners to practice our daring moves.

Westmoreland Avenue was about a mile from my house. A handful of kids, mostly older than me, hung out there together. Being the youngest, I'm sure I was more often the young pest from the other neighborhood. There was Deron, Todd, Darby, a guy named Benji, and Tim. I looked up to these guys. To this day, Deron and I remain friends. I speak to Todd and Darby on occasion, and am not sure what became of the other guys.

Like clockwork, every day over that summer I would wake up, play guitar for a few hours, and then head over to their street to ride our bikes or do tricks while listening to a boom box. No pocket-size iPods back then. The bigger, the better.

By this time, the '80s hard-rock movement was the in thing in suburbia, and we had stacks of cassette tapes from Quiet Riot, Van Halen, Mötley Crüe, Ratt, and Twisted Sister, to name a few. The one kid I thought was the coolest at the time was Todd. He played guitar and was quiet and mysterious, but more than anything, he seemed to have his pulse on the music coming out of LA more than anyone I knew. He would show up with tapes of bands none of us had ever heard of. He was the messenger, oftentimes delivering us the next big thing before we knew what it was.

If memory serves me correctly, Todd had taken a summer vacation to LA, and on this late-August day he showed up with a bag of fresh new music. Among the tapes was one called *Look What the Cat Dragged In*. The cover caused a lot of controversy back in the day. It had four guys with extremely wild hair and makeup on, but to be honest with you, I never thought about it. Every band wore makeup, every band had a similar image, but this group did do it bigger and better. The band was Poison. On that hot August day, my life was about to change in so many ways.

Todd put the tape in and "Cry Tough" came blaring through the speakers.

First the drumbeat. Then the guitar riff, and

then the whole thing exploded with energy. I was sold instantly. The opening lyric spoke to me.

Remember the nights we sat
And talked about all our dreams

I wasn't a songwriter yet, but I wish I'd written those words. I was living them.

I think I was born a hopeless romantic. I'd always take sitting on the hood of a car talking to a girl about what we might become one day over going to a party and drinking till I puked.

The opening lyric of "Cry Tough" was clearly written about the life I was leading; finally someone was talking to me. To this day I love the LA scene of that era, but I was a bit too young then to really be inspired or excited by the sexual lyrical content that most of the music was about. While I lived and died for Van Halen at the time, it was purely Eddie's guitar that I craved. I didn't care one bit if anyone but David Lee Roth ruled the streets at night as proclaimed in their song "Atomic Punk." I couldn't figure out if "Panama" was a place, a car, or a girl. (Later I found out he wrote that on purpose to evoke the very kind of confusion I was having. "Panama" is still to this day in my top three for my desert-island playlist.)

I couldn't relate to Nikki Sixx, Mötley Crüe's main songwriter, when he penned "Shout at The

Devil." I didn't believe in the devil, nor did I care. I wasn't mad at the devil and certainly wasn't going to shout at him. Every one of their songs that wasn't about sex was singing about switchblades and that just wasn't my thing; however, as I got a little older, it did all seem super cool.

The music of the era was powerful. I was sold on the energy and the sound. But Poison was different. While they made the trek to Hollywood to make it, they weren't from the West Coast or some big city. Those guys were from a small town in Pennsylvania—just one state away from Virginia. Maybe that's why I could relate. Another East Coast band, Twisted Sister, had my attention too with their songs "I Wanna Rock" and "We're Not Gonna Take It." Long before the rappers had their East/West Coast rivalries, rock and roll had similar differences. Us east coasters had Twisted Sister, Kiss, and Bon Jovi, the west coast had Van Halen, Quit Riot, and Ratt. The difference was they just didn't shoot each other.

"Cry Tough" had struck such a nerve with me that I begged Todd to let me take the tape home that night. He agreed, and I played that tape over and over again. Suddenly, the second verse came screaming out at me.

Life ain't no easy ride,
At least that's what I'm told.

But sometimes the rainbow, baby,
 Is better than the pot of gold.

And there it was. The single most defining lyric
of my life, to this very day. It's been my go-to
mantra for everything. Don't get me wrong, there
are thousands of lyrics that are inspiring. I could
write a book on them, but none changed me like
"Cry Tough." The only song that even comes a
close second to touching me is "Right Now" from
Van Halen. Those lyrics were life changing for me
also.

"Cry Tough" gave me validation to be poor, to
struggle, to *not* make it. It gave me permission to
chase my dreams at all cost. Eventually I listened to
the whole album and loved it. Poison was cooler
than cool. I was going to spread the word, and that
I did. Day after day. Month after month. Year after
year.

I played "Cry Tough" in two different high
school talent shows over the years. And everyone I
met, I shoved Poison down their throat. I carried
that lyric with me every day. I knew the tales of
poverty that are intertwined with the struggle to
succeed in the music business. While many people
have a lucky charm they take with them to
meetings, events, or where they think they may
need a little help, I had "Cry Tough." I guess, in
short. it became my personal anthem. I'd play it in

the car before my band had a show. I'd play it in my room before trying out new band members. If you were going to audition for our band, you had to learn that song. It just meant everything to me. As I got older and the reality of that whole being poor to make it big thing started to sink in, I relied on the message.

Later that year, I got to see Poison, as they were the support act for Ratt. I'd seen a few concerts and the opening bands always sucked. I was a huge Ratt fan, but let me tell you, Poison blew them away.

I didn't know what to expect. I had rallied about eight of my buddies to go with me to the concert. I put my faith in the fact that this band would blow my friends away. That night we all left with Poison T-shirts, not a single Ratt shirt, if that tells you anything.

When Poison came out with a new album, "Nothin' But a Good Time" became an instant anthem, and they were becoming a household name. This time they would tour as the opening band for former Van Halen singer David Lee Roth.

Now, Van Halen is my favorite band of all time. At this point, we all thought David Lee Roth would go down in history as our generation's Robert Plant or Elvis Presley. Well, we were dead wrong.

That night I saw Poison open up for David Lee Roth, what I actually saw was the star who would basically walk over and take the front-man-of-a-generation crown off the head of David Lee Roth and emerge as the long-lasting king of all things rock and roll. That man is the single biggest rock-and-roll legend of my generation, an international superstar, a reality TV icon, a household name, and the best friend and teacher I've ever had—Bret Michaels.

Around 1992, when Poison's guitarist, C.C. DeVille, took a break from the band, Capitol Records was looking to replace him with one of the already known LA guitar heroes. There was a local Virginia guy named Michael Fath who was making waves nationally as one of these guitar-hero types. He was even featured on the cover of a huge guitar magazine. He had managed to talk to Poison, or their management, but from his own mouth he was too old for the gig. I was only nineteen at the time, but I asked Michael for the number so I could take a crack at the audition. He was kind enough to pass on the info, and as far as I was concerned, I was going to be in Poison. The job was meant for me.

When I called, I was kindly told there was a deadline for audition tapes—which was only two days away. I had nothing to give them. I didn't have a demo, but that didn't stop me. I rushed home and cut one on my Fostex four-track recorder. I put on my coolest rock outfit. Put makeup on, since that was the in thing to do back then, and took some pictures that I had developed at the one-hour-photo shop. Still in full makeup and rock gear, I sped to FedEx with my promo package. I'll never forget that ride, because I got pulled over for speeding.

Back then, being a guy performing in a nightclub with eyeliner on was one thing; being pulled over in Manassas, Virginia, at 4 p.m. was another. The cop wasn't too kind. He practically barked at me, "Why are you wearing makeup?"

When I told the officer that I was auditioning for one of my favorite bands, his attitude changed. Maybe he knew how ridiculous it was that I believed I could make it and felt sorry for me, assuming I'd be depressed in a few weeks when it didn't happen. Whatever the reason, that officer not only let me go without a ticket, but he wished me luck. I made it to FedEx before closing. The package was on its way, and all I had to do was go home and wait for my phone call. The one telling me when to come to LA and play guitar for Poison.

That call never came. I did receive a phone call thanking me for the tape and was told that while everyone liked it, they were looking for someone a little older who had an already established name in the world of guitar heroics.

For some reason, the sadness and the depression never came. Because I knew that . . . wait for it . . .

Sometimes the rainbow
Is better than the pot of gold.

I had done something none of my peers had
done yet, or even dreamed about doing. We were
all too young to start auditioning for pro bands. We
were barely able to poke our heads out of our local
scene, but I opened that door. It was an important
part of my journey. I may not have gotten the pot of
gold, but I had a great story. I truly believe in the
end our worth is really not money, or anything like
that. It's our story. The choices we make. The steps
we take. Even the wrong turns that seem to take us
back further than where we originally started. As of
that day, I began to have bigger and better stories
than anyone else I knew. The sheer thought of
sending an audition tape to Poison positioned me a
bit higher than the rest of my peers. Not only was it
impressive to them, but I'd pushed myself a little
and felt rewarded by the outcome. Not so much
different than going to the gym and besting
yourself one day after the next.

The irony of all this, for those who don't know
me, is that my big break, my pot of gold so to speak,
finally came when I became Bret Michaels's guitar
player in his solo band. That was ten years ago, and
I'm still the guy to his right rocking out in front of
sold-out crowds all over the world.

Because of Bret, I have seen the world. I have

lived out every single one of my wildest rock-and-roll dreams and lots more, from flying on his private jet to performing at the Playboy Mansion and every decadent rock-and-roll luxury and fantasy you can think of. I could go on for days, but that, like my alien theories, is a book all its own.

The music business and what happens in it is somewhat of a mystery, whether it be how to succeed in it; or what happens backstage, on the bus, in business meetings, or at the homes of rock stars; how much money they make, or how it is that they can do whatever they want and seemingly get away with it. All those things are somewhat shrouded in secrecy. The short and simple answer I give anyone who asks: my pot of gold is that I have the answers to those questions. I've lived it. I know all the things that I ever dreamed and wondered about. I know what it's like to play in front of more than a hundred thousand people. I know what it's like to perform on a hit song. I know what it's like to be in a number-one video. I know what it's like to receive accolades from the music industry elite. And the reason for my success is because Bret Michaels, with those simple words, inspired me to never give up, then actually turned out to be the guy at the finish line to welcome me across.

Bret has become so much more to me—a brother, a teacher, a mentor, and a friend. There is so much more to him than anyone will ever know.

He's provided me with an education not only in rock and roll, but also in life, finance, and most importantly, loyalty. He taught me what it means to be a true friend and to have one. I got that real wrong for a lot of years. I can honestly say that if I had to go to battle and pick one man to have my back, it would be Bret.

From day one, music is all I've known. I truly eat, breathe, and sleep this stuff. It's given me everything; it *is* everything to me. I've traveled the world. I've done every single thing I've ever dreamed of and more, and done every bit of it with a six string in my hand. I still get as excited today as the very first time I ever heard "Jump" from Van Halen, and every single night on stage when Bret strums the first chords to "Every Rose Has Its Thorn," I'm instantly taken back to the moment in 1988 when I first heard the song coming through the speakers of my Sanyo stereo. I'm blessed to have been able to do all of this.

***

You might not often think of a lyric as a tool to teach your children, but I have passed on those lines from "Cry Tough" to my kids. Already, media has influenced them, and money means more to them than it should. My oldest son talks about being rich and famous. It's a hard lesson to explain that fame for the sake of being famous is purely disgusting, and if that's what you're after, then your life will be empty and shallow even if your pockets are full.

My oldest son is truly innocent in his attitude though, and has aspirations of being the next George Lucas. He wants to be recognized for doing something great, but he wants it to happen overnight, and he wants the kind of money Bret has in his bank account when he doesn't even have a bank account yet. We've had some heart-to-hearts about enjoying the journey, taking it in, smelling the roses, and that sometimes the rainbow is better than the pot of gold.

It's a valuable lesson, for sure.

Not that there are winners or losers, but if there were, I'm without a doubt the biggest winner of all time, at least in my own mind.

Who gets to be in a band with one of their heroes? I often joke with Bret that while he has mansions, jets, and fancy cars (his Bentley is by far my favorite of his personal assets, and he's kind enough to let me take it back and forth across I-10 between LA and Arizona at lawless speeds), plus more money than his children's children will ever need, that I'm the luckier one of us because I get to be in a band with him. He doesn't get to be in a band with one of his heroes, like Steven Tyler, Angus Young, or Ronnie Van Zandt. However, I also remind him that he's superseded his own heroes. Those guys will go down in rock-and-roll history, no doubt, but Bret himself will go down in American history.

What I'm trying to say is that I'm the luckiest guy I know. Through an amazing course of strange events such as the ones I've explained through the chapters in this book, I found myself molded into exactly who I needed to be to get exactly where I wanted to go. And as I searched through my memories and experiences to bring them to you, I learned that we are all guided by a higher power and that those tools to help us achieve our dreams are hidden in the strangest places, yet right in front us. Maybe, just maybe, those who don't achieve their dreams just didn't look inside themselves to see the unique road map we all seem to possess.

To sum up my personal journey right down to this very moment:

THE RAINBOW IS THE POT OF GOLD.

Epilogue

At first, years ago, this book was just a personal outlet. A journal I used as a way to express myself through the demise of my marriage. Sometimes it was my way of being my own therapist. Other times, it was my way of trying to explain to the ex why I'd failed. These pages were long social-media posts that I ultimately decided not to post.

It became a project that I assumed I would never finish. Truth be told, I've started several books—fiction and nonfiction. I've begun a collection of stories about the music industry, a how-to-succeed-in-the-music-biz book, even my own Star Wars novel. I'd come out of the gate fast and hard, excited to tell the story, but being a songwriter I was accustomed to finishing a single page of words, many that repeat themselves several times, and then being done.

To go from songwriter to book author is like being a sprinter and suddenly running a marathon. Writing this book has been another milestone. As I began to understand the process of writing and *finishing* a book, I became more comfortable and confident as a writer.

As with the other times I sat down to write, the first four or five chapters flowed out of me almost as if it were someone else doing the work through my body. I started to believe there was a higher purpose for this book.

Trust me, at no point had I ever thought that a collection of stories from Bret Michaels's guitar player's strange but good childhood was anything anyone would care about. A lot of times it seemed shallow and even egotistical to continue. Yet for years, my friends and family have encouraged me to write a book. I'm sure they were all talking about a book of rock-and-roll decadence. After all, I've had a pretty amazing experience over the last twenty-five years. But not so unlike that scene in *Wayne's World 2* where Jim Morrison tells Wayne to put on a concert and people will come, the more I wrote, the more I wanted to write and share these stories, with the notion that if I write, people will read.

But that's scary. These are personal accounts, and although the reason I'm sharing them is for others to learn that it's okay to dig a little deeper to understand who you are, some people may take joy in my failures and the darker parts of my life.

I shared the first chapters with a few people, and got a lot of positive feedback, the most common comments being that they appreciate how willing I seemed to let the light shine on my darkest secrets, and how I seemed to remember in vivid detail the things that most of us try to bury.

I will reiterate this disclaimer: these stories are as I remember them.

Like I said in the beginning of this book—perception is everything. I am certain that almost every person I have mentioned will have a slightly different version of these events—if they remember them at all. This is *my* truth. My reality. I'm grateful to be able to share these parts of me with anyone who will listen. However, it did become very hard at times. I was forced to dig into my memories, and just reliving those moments so I could tell these stories became traumatic at times.

Many of the chapters are pretty short. The fact is, when I sat down to write them, they poured out of me in a matter of minutes. What amazed me was the effort it took to open the MacBook and actually sit down to type them. Over my five and a half years of writing this, I probably only spent a fraction of the time typing compared to the time I spent thinking and brainstorming about the content. There were several moments on countless plane rides all over the world where I hunted for my own mental scars, then had to decipher the message and decide if it would mean anything to anyone else. People who know me know that I usually hate the amount of time I have to spend in airports because of my job, but the truth is, those plane rides are where I've found I can be at one with myself. No cell phones. No interruptions. Just me and my brain.

Once the concept of the book became that of motivation and inspiration, it laid another stress on me. I needed each story to somehow be relatable to every reader, at least in theory. While I wanted my stories to be so unique that everyone smiled, laughed, or shrugged in disbelief as they read, I needed to tell the stories in a way that made people connect with their own moments that changed their lives.

There would be weeks, sometimes months, when I would wake up knowing what I wanted to write, but I just couldn't do it. The same voice in my head that was forcing me to write this book seemed to also be telling me "not today."

Whoever or whatever drove me to write all this must have understood that the stories needed to simmer like a crockpot of emotion. One chapter led to the next thought. Sometimes that little idea would seem meaningless, but once I let my guard down and spent the time swimming in my own history, it would seem to come together. This book consumed my mind. At times the sheer thought I put into it, the dredging up of childhood trauma, physically exhausted me. Strangely though, even as I walked through some of the darkness of my past, my blood boiled with excitement to finish it.

I'm still not 100 percent sure why I was so driven to write this book, but I hope one day I meet the spirit that drove me to do it. Or maybe I'll meet one person whose life will be touched by what I've shared.

I'm certain it's made me a much better human being. I like myself a whole lot more today than I did the day I sat down to write chapter one. Part of my intent is to inspire, or to challenge people to soul-search, and certainly to get them to love, care, and be cautious with the impressionable minds of children. The ego in me, the ever-present Leo, dreams of a movement much like the movie *Pay It Forward*. I certainly don't need my name attached to it. After all, when we are all just light floating in the universe, I won't be Pete Evick, but I'd love to think that after forty years of overthinking I can or am supposed to change the world in some way, if not influence it in a good way just a little. I hope the words filling these pages may be enough to alter just one person's mind, and in turn maybe that person can change another person's mind, and so, in some small way, I did my part in nudging our human evolution on the path of higher self-awareness, unconditional love, tolerance, and acceptance.

If my stories inspire a memory of something similar in your life, or help you make a correlation between a moment and a recurring emotion, then I have done what I set out to do. Either way, if you've made it this far, I'm truly grateful and humbled that you took time out of your own life to read about mine.

Thank you so very much.

~ * ~

**If you enjoyed this book, please take a
moment to leave a review on Amazon, Barnes
and Noble or Goodreads.**

Acknowledgments

Thanks to Keith Sarna for working his magic on the book cover, and to Cyndi Stephens and Tina Lu for their photographs.

To all of the musicians and songwriters I've mentioned in this body of work, thanks for the inspiration and education I've received through your work. And to Daniel A. Weiss, Attorney at Law, for the legwork to get all the clearance needed to add the lyrics to the songs that had special impact in my life.

While it's been more than half a decade that Kristen and I have been apart, I wanted readers to know that we get along better than ever. And while we know that things are better this way, we celebrate the good that came from our decade together. I feel we are unique because we still manage to spend our children's birthdays and Christmas together as a family. We agreed on a very relaxed joint-custody agreement, which basically says that when I'm home, the children are welcome to be with me. I'm fortunate that there has never been a division of "Tuesdays and Thursdays and every other weekend" type of thing. I understand it works for some people, but not me. I'd be in prison if someone tried to regulate the amount of time I got to see my boys. While I've come to the conclusion that Kristen and I will never again agree, if we even ever did, about the world and how to exist in it, she is an amazing and loving mother to my children and is truly a kind and innocent soul. I'm grateful for all we've done together.

Thank you Nancy Naigle for the patience and encouragement.

About the Author

Pete Evick is still a Virginia boy at heart with tight ties to his hometown of Manassas. He is a multitalented musician/producer who, in addition to playing guitar in the Bret Michaels Band, has also served as a co-songwriter, producer, mixer, and musical director for the group, and his own band, EVICK. A man with a true entrepreneurial spirit, he pursues his own projects, which have included the conception of an all digital record company called Potomac Records which has been turned over to his close high-school friend, Mike Bailey, and a new environmentally conscious candle company also based in Virginia called Shining Sol Candle Company.

Although Pete is an award-winning producer, his biggest role in life remains that of being the best father he can to his two boys.

Stay up to date on releases, appearances, and news on Facebook (Official Pete Evick), Twitter (@PeteEvick), and his website, PeteEvick.com.

Check out other work by Pete Evick

The Music: *Available on iTunes and Amazon*

 Reflections

 Anachronism

Sunset to Sunset

The Candles:

www.ShiningSol.com
#ShareTheLight

Sign up for Pete's newsletter to be the first to hear about upcoming promotions, and events at http://www.PeteEvick.com.

32443850R00124

Made in the USA
San Bernardino, CA
08 April 2016